Bothered and Bewildered

By the same author and published by Bloomsbury

Journeying Out: A New Approach to Christian Mission
ISBN 978–08264-8096–5

Beyond the Good Samaritan
ISBN 978–08264-7141–3

Bothered and Bewildered

Enacting Hope in Troubled Times

Ann Morisy

BLOOMSBURY

LONDON • NEW DELHI • NEW YORK • SYDNEY

Bloomsbury Continuum
An imprint of Bloomsbury Publishing Plc

50 Bedford Square   1385 Broadway
London   New York
WC1B 3DP   NY10018
UK   USA

www.bloomsbury.com

First published in 2009 by the Continuum International Publishing Group Ltd
Reprinted by Bloomsbury Continuum 2013, 2014

British Library Cataloguing-in-Publication Data
A Catalogue record for this publication is available from the British Library.

ISBN: 978-1-8470-6480-6

Library of Congress Cataloging-in-Publication Data
A Catalog record for this book is available from the Library of Congress.

Designed and typeset by Free Range Book Design & Production
Printed and Bound in Great Britain

This book is dedicated to Candy Torres,
a pioneer of enacted hope in difficult times

Contents

Acknowledgements

I should like to thank Judith Daley, Simon Grigg, David Heywood and Margaret Kesterton for helping me with this book. Thanks are also due to Caroline Chartres at Continuum for her encouragement with the task.

I also express my appreciation to the staff and students of the YMCA George Williams College in Canning Town for pioneering commitment to reflective and honest practice.

Treatise

We are living in troubled times and people have become bothered and bewildered.

When people are bothered and bewildered, great caution is needed because our instinctive response is scapegoating and death-dealing.

Christian teaching and practice need to take account of this potential for scapegoating and death-dealing and are especially relevant here because Jesus brings an end to the need for a scapegoat.

The unique capacity of Christianity to help people rise above death-dealing inclinations makes it urgent that we share our faith, but this mission imperative must be combined with pastoral care.

It's imperative that we don't lose sight of hope, but simply to declaim or assert hope isn't enough: we have to *enact* it. Enacted hope consists of tiny micro actions and graced actions that point to the reality of God's design for his creation.

In a time when we are bothered and bewildered, a vital resource is the capacity for reflectiveness on the part of those both inside the Church and outside it.

The J-Curve graph alerts us to the danger that, when things are bad, there is a risk of taking shortcuts to avoid the challenge of changing our ways.

One reason we are so bothered and bewildered is because we have invested so much in the economy of scarcity that we find it hard to believe that there is also an economy of abundance.

In his actions and teaching, Jesus shows us how we can participate in this economy of abundance.

Others are also discovering the viability of the economy of abundance, in particular those concerned with positive psychology, which endorses long-established faith practices and the health-giving aspects of having a faith.

Positive psychology underlines that our capacity for wellbeing is not just to do with our genes and circumstances, but that there is vast scope for *intentional activities,* even when confronted by the direst circumstances.

Faith practices have an exceptional track record of helping people – especially those in dire circumstances (including addictions) – to rise above those circumstances and engage in life-enhancing *intentional activity.*

In the economy of abundance intentional activities which express generosity and compassion generate a cascade of positive outcomes.

The ability to make sense of our actions within a larger frame gives vital motivation to embrace the intentional activity that enables us to resist being *victims* of troublesome circumstances.

This relevance and transformational power of our Christian faith, especially in troubled times, make it urgent to build a church which enables people to engage with the coaching that Jesus gives in how to live, rather than emphasising 'hard-to-believe' formulaic faith.

1 Dystopia ... the End of a Hope-filled Future

As I walk past the lines of horse chestnut trees I see the leaves have turned brown, and many that have fallen weeks and weeks ahead of autumn. I notice how the bark has split on many of the trees and a sticky sap exudes. Yes, these trees like so many horse chestnuts are infested by tiny leaf boring moths and also affected by bleeding canker ... I wonder whether the local authority knows about the problems? And then I speculate that the parks department won't be in a position to tackle such a large scale problem in a way that sustains rather than demolishes. In my dystopian mood I foresee the chainsaw working overtime as one after another the trees are brought down because of health and safety concerns that large branches may fall. The splendid avenue of trees that had given pleasure over the century will disappear and be impossible to replace ... And then the question as to why these magnificent trees have succumbed now to these tiny moths and canker, and my thoughts turn to London pollution and global warming. This dismal spiral is made real each day as I mundanely walk the dog.[1]

I grew up with the expression 'As old as a conker tree'. Conker, or should I say horse chestnut trees, can be two hundred years old and they are tall and statuesque, they are likely to be the biggest and strongest trees in our parklands. That's how it is on Streatham Common. Each morning I walk the dog on the Common, and walk

---

1   The current assessment as to what is happening to horse chestnut trees is that they are infected by Ohridella: 'in only four years clouds of this rare little insect have romped through most of England'. The bleeding canker is an airborne infection and is deadly on trees up to the age of about twenty-five. 'It is a valid reason for felling a chestnut, whereas the insect-attackers are not,' Robin Lane Fox, 'Troubled Trees', *Financial Times*, 4/5 October 2008.

along a path lined by mighty horse chestnut trees, but rather than being awed by their stature my heart sinks. I get caught up in a dystopian perspective. I start to ponder how the future is likely to be worse than the present. It may begin with something small, but it grows bigger and bigger and more and more dreadful. Each concern branches out into a host of other concerns. Each item in a newscast can trigger a dismal assemblage of thoughts which emphasise our inability to put things right after they have gone wrong. Instead of confidence in science, technology and human organisation, the opposite begins to dominate our thoughts as we see not invention and innovation, but gridlocks and malfunctions.

It is not the best way of ensuring people continue to turn over to the next page by listing more and more things to worry about. My purpose is not to add to already high levels of anxiety, but I know that what follows will do this. For this I apologise, although in defence, the list of concerns that will be presented are probably in line with most news broadcasts. Others may find themselves protesting that I misrepresent reality with so many dismal assessments and wish to counter my miserable list with the fact that joy is still at large in the world. Let us thank God for that. It is important that when we are bothered and bewildered we do not lose confidence in the resilience, enterprise and imagination of the human and holy spirit.

It is always hard to judge the appropriateness of our perspective on the signs of the times. It is as easy to get carried away with a dystopian mood as it is to plough on regardless of major changes in attitude – and reality. So will the current dismal mood pass because is it just a temporary state, no worse than other periods in history … or have we entered into something new, never before so serious? And who can be trusted to tell of how it is? 'Experts' used to be the people that we turned to for a measured response to counter the sound and fury from the media. But now it seems that on more and more issues, among them climate change and the financial crisis, the experts now seem more apocalyptic than the public.

The speed with which confidence in progress has crumbled has been so fast that many dictionaries have yet to carry reference to the word 'dystopian'.[2] The first record of the word being used was

---

2   Dystopia might be understood as the opposite of utopia, which means 'any ideal place or state', and was coined by Sir Thomas More from the

by John Stuart Mill in 1868, and it is an idea that has been captured by many science-fiction writers. Aldous Huxley's *Brave New World* and George Orwell's *Nineteen Eighty-Four* are probably the best known. This genre of science fiction depicts an imaginary society in which social or technological trends result in a much diminished quality of life or a collapse of values. To these books must be added the film of the Anthony Burgess novel *A Clockwork Orange*, which, rather than focusing on dysfunctional government and governmental agencies, depicts the absence of government control allowing people themselves to cause the dystopian chaos.

This evaporation of confidence in progress, and the sudden foolishness of assuming that things can only get better, ushers in a *post* 'postmodern' period, characterised by the chill of anxiety and fear. And it has been sudden: almost overnight two centuries of upbeat optimism and sturdy confidence that things could and would get better has unravelled. But whilst for some the word 'dystopian' may be new, those who play video games are forever contemplating dystopias. Even though in the culture of video gaming 'last week' makes for 'old', there is a consistent theme of how the world has gone wrong.

> *A world gone wrong ... BioShock: The player enters the underwater city of Rapture, where only the 'Splicers' – citizens with severe mental and physical problems caused by excessive ADAM (a mutagen) use – are left, scavenging throughout the city, whilst the remaining non-mutated humans have barricaded themselves in the few remaining undamaged areas, although most of these people have also become mentally unstable or dangerous in some way. The aim of the game? To take on the role of Jack and single-handedly negotiate the terrors of life gone wrong.*

PEOPLE SCREW UP

Ken Levine, who was the originator of *BioShock*, in an interview on the gaming website IGN, commenting on what

---

Greek meaning 'no place' i.e. an imagined place. If More had intended the meaning 'a good place', the Greek would be eutopia. So strictly speaking dystopian is not the opposite of utopian!

influenced the game's story and setting, said, 'I have my useless liberal arts degree, so I've read stuff from Ayn Rand[3] and George Orwell, and all the sort of utopian and dystopian writings of the 20th century, which I've found really fascinating.'[4] As well as referring to the impact of *Nineteen Eighty-Four*, Levine also noted the film *Logan's Run* which provides yet another illustration of societies that have 'really interesting ideas screwed up by the fact that we're people'. *BioShock* is immensely popular (at least it is this week!) and, like so many games, it punches home the message that 'really interesting ideas get screwed-up by the fact we're people'. This miserable assessment of human potential and the need for a hero to rescue 'people gone wrong', makes for a raw theology that is pulsed into the subconscious of young men, because mostly it is young men who 'game'.

This seeking for a hero who can rescue humankind often accompanies a dystopian perspective. Wherever there is a sense of things going to the dogs there quickly follows the desire for a hero or leader who can perform the great act of rescue. The Psalmist repeatedly sings of this longing, confident that the Lord will not let a foot slip, nor allow the sun to harm us by day and will keep us from all harm, both now and for evermore.[5] Well that's a relief: those who put their faith in God have nothing to fear from dystopian eruptions ... except that our faith, as exemplified by Jesus, the incarnate Son of God, does not permit such distancing from struggle and dismay. Salvation is not to be confused with escape. Religious reassurance of eternal safety that protects the faithful from earthly struggle is a heresy. But it is a very tempting heresy.

Christians have to be wary of disdain for a world 'gone wrong', especially when this combines with the desire to escape. Such

---

3   Ayn Rand advocated rational individualism and laissez-faire capitalism, actively rejecting altruism and religion (objectivism). Her many works include *Anthem* (1938), a dystopian vision of a futuristic society where collectivism has triumphed, and *Atlas Shrugged* (1957), involving a dystopian America where industrialists and other creative individuals go on strike and retreat to a mountain hideaway to build an alternative economy.

4   D.C. Perry, 'The Influence of Literature and Myth in Videogames', IGN, 26 May 2006.

5   Paraphrase of Psalm 121.

preoccupation with escape and self-preservation Tolkein bluntly describes as *desertion*.[6] This is not about a temporary withdrawal in order to return with renewed vigour, but rather the creation of a 'fortress of (the) imagination'.[7] However, this utter craving to escape calls for compassion rather than belittling, because when we are bothered and bewildered, we are at risk of escapist, self-serving theological strategies. When worried about the future – and our future in particular, there is a danger that any ideology, religious or otherwise, is seized upon as a 'way out' or 'way through'. In particular, in fearful dystopian times, people (that's all of us) seek heroes who can find a way through and bring salvation. At first glance this desire for rescue may appear a glorious mission opportunity, with the field ripened for harvest with plentiful souls ready to enter the sheepfold. However, this is a time to be very alert to the ease with which religion and ideology can become 'furious' and fuel destructive and death-dealing passions. Anxiety feeds the need for right answers. However, 'right answers' fed by unacknowledged anxiety are brittle, and when challenged by those who see things differently can prompt intense emotionalism, and things can turn nasty.

The raw theology carried by so many video games, that people 'screw up', has to be pondered long and hard if our dystopian fears are to be addressed rather than compounded by brittle right-answerism. Unless honest thinking is embraced, the fierce reactiveness that fosters furious religion will prevail. When we are bothered and bewildered it is doubly important that our thinking and reflecting are courageous and honest. And in particular it is necessary to avoid two 'quasi' intellectual habits:

• The assumption that it is possible to impose solutions on people as a method of rekindling hope. Virtuous behaviour cannot be

---

6   J.R.R. Tolkien, *On Fairy Stories, in Tree and Leaf*, London: Unwin Books, 1964, p. 54; cited in Christopher Mark Perrott, '"*In the city, but not of it*": Exploring the Roots of Evangelicalism's Uneasy Relationship with Holistic Urban Mission', unpublished dissertation MTh, Spurgeon's College, University of Wales, 2005, p. 15.

7   P.J. Lee, *Against the Protestant Gnostics*, Oxford: Oxford University Press, 1987, p. 140; cited in Perrott, p. 15.

enforced. Whilst people might be forced to behave well, virtuous behaviour, enforcement does not foster hope that can counter dismay.

• The habit of thinking in terms of 'them and us': the raw theology of video gaming – *that things get screwed up by the fact we're people,* leaves no room for distancing analyses that put the blame on some and ignore the culpability of others. Solzhenitsyn noted how the dividing line between good and evil cuts through the heart of every human being, and this reality allows for no exemption. Christian theology does not divide the world into 'bad guys' and 'us'; rather, we are all in need of a saviour.

'Them and us' thinking invariably involves thinking in clichés, and the problem with clichés is that they do our thinking for us, and channel, and therefore constrain, our thoughts and emotions. So the 'them' are the slackers, the immoral, the wreckers and the disrupters of the peace, and the 'us' are the upholders of standards of decency and hard work and democracy. This cartoon-like depiction of baddies and goodies serves to legitimate government measures to punish 'others' (especially migrants and asylum seekers and young people) and feeds demands for greater conformity and homogeneity. Such an analysis results in the conclusion that the world would be a better place if everyone was like us, but in a globalising, fragmenting world the very opposite dynamics prevail.

MAKE WAY FOR GLOBALISATION

Globalisation means that those who move into 'my' place are less and less likely to be people like me, as the gusts of powerful economic forces bring movements of people across national boundaries. Laurie Green describes globalisation as what happens when 'Powerful economic forces combine with the radically new technologies ... changing the nature, functions and powers of the State, leading to vast migrations of people, the fragmentation and dispersal of manufacturing and construction systems, and producing the new hyper-urbanisation of the globe.'[8] Globalisation,

8   L. Green, *The Impact of the Global: An Urban Theology*, New City: UTU, 2000, p. 11.

whilst not dystopian in itself, adds to discomfort and anxiety levels: no longer are neighbours likely to be like us, and throughout human history strangers have always prompted fear.

Globalisation also refers to a process through which national economies become more open, and thus more subject to supranational economic influences, and less amenable to national control. And this brings with it another frustration: the habit of calling on the *government* to do something to sort things out now belongs to the past. The global nature of economic activity has led 'government' to be 'hollowed out'. This is a term coined by Castells[9] to describe the enfeeblement of the governments of nation states in the face of global financial systems. A major factor in the economic turmoil that began in 2008 was that the regulation of financial systems has been in the hands of national regulators, and crossborder cooperation to achieve regulation of a global financial system had still to be fashioned.

Governments can scarcely ease our bothered and bewildered state when multinational companies can be bigger than nation states, and have the ultimate sanction to move elsewhere if a national government should dare to increase tax on profits or high-earning executives. And there is more: with globalisation some of the traditional trappings of the nation state loose their previous legitimacy. An example of this is how the armed forces of a nation are no longer assured of support from the populace. So, in a globalising world, I may be a citizen of a country that claims legitimacy in directing smart bombs on my brothers and sisters in my country of origin. Loyalty to a nation and its representatives becomes problematic when people have roots in other nations, and the ease of travel and communication makes it possible to maintain those roots.

There are multiple dynamics that give energy to globalisation: technological developments that feed the 'information' revolution and the world-wide web leading to the rapid flow of ideas, rapid ways of transport of people and things; the growth of disinhibiting environments[10] of multi-channel TV, chatrooms, computer games

---

9   M. Castells, *The Rise of the Network Society*, Oxford: Blackwell, 1996.
10   One of my favourite cartoons from the *New Yorker* illustrates this idea of 'disinhibition' very well. A dog is sitting at the computer tapping

and social networking. The interconnectedness that results has unsurpassed social consequences which we mostly welcome or consider to be unproblematic developments. But somewhere deep down runs the fear of the rarely acknowledged addictiveness of such a constructed world.

Globalisation brings with it 'popular' cultures of consumption. Icons of the 'shared' global experience are transmitted around the world – it may be trainers or jeans or iPods or Coke or Pizza Hut or watching the same TV programmes, clumsily dubbed. Standardisation, homogeneity and cultural imperialism are all complaints laid at the door of globalisation, and against which we, governments and nations appear to have scarce defence. And so we lament that town centres all look the same, or that they are no longer viable as the marketing of these consumer goods calls for smart malls or quick-to-construct consumer sheds to house carpets, kitchens, toys and electrical stuff, with acres of car parking since we now shop with a car rather than a shopping bag. Or at least we did.

The Italian sociologist Luciano Gallino points to the formation of a 'world economy' as the engine of globalisation. He defines globalisation as 'The acceleration and intensification of the process of formation of a world economy which is emerging as a single system operating in real time.'[11] Until the current collapse of economies around the world[12] Gallino's focus on economic processes might have seemed partial, but his analysis has proved prescient. Whilst he acknowledges the technological underpinning of globalisation, he puts the spotlight on the world superpowers, and the international financial institutions that they sponsor, and the loose regulation of global markets, which he anticipates will all lead to an implosion, and the whole system will collapse in on itself. Gallino was writing this in 2001.

---

away at the keyboard; he boasts to the dog looking up at him in admiration 'Nobody knows you're a dog on the internet.'

11 L. Gallino, 'Globalizzazione e sviluppo della rete', Proceedings of the Congress Mappe del '900, Rimini 22–24 November 2001, *I viaggi di Erodoto*, supplement, vol. 14, no. 43–4 (2001), p. 125.

12 At the time of writing the crash of stockmarkets and the re-aligning of long-established investment banks is so current it remains to be given a name. The current descriptor 'the credit crunch' scarcely seems adequate to describe the extensiveness and depth of the fallout that is being experienced.

And here we have it: the day-to-day impact of globalisation on the things that are marketed and the ways they are marketed is one thing, the fact that neighbours are no longer like us is another, and then the coup de grâce – the financial structures to which everyone is tied implode. There is a sense that the current financial meltdown and economic downturn do not so much signal that a crisis has begun, but rather that they show just how much chaos there is below the surface of this globalising process.

DECADENT VAGABONDS

There are huge human and social consequences of our shrinking and homogenising world. Bauman suggests that a consequence of postmodernity and globalisation is *Life in Fragments*.[13] He suggests that the loss of any metanarrative or 'big story', around which shared perspectives can develop, has resulted in more and more polarity and segregation. Bauman suggests that globalisation, rather than bringing greater tolerance of diversity in its wake, moves people towards a new expression of tribalism. This *neo-tribalism* gets expressed through choice of fashion, leisure, lifestyle or ethnic-religious origin, which all become possible within diasporic[14] global networks. The desire for strong identification with one's own distinctive neo-tribe is, according to Bauman, a response to disorientation, fear and insecurity.

Bauman describes the individual lost in the hubbub of conflicting noises as a 'vagabond',

> a pilgrim without a destination; a nomad without an itinerary ... (who) ... journeys through unstructured space; like a wanderer in the desert, who only knows of such trails as are marked with his own footprints, and blown off again by the wind the moment he passes, the vagabond structures the site he happens to occupy at the moment, only to dismantle the structure again as he leaves. Each successive spacing is local and temporary.[15]

---

13 Z. Bauman, *Life in Fragments*, Oxford: Blackwell, 1995.
14 The dispersion of a people from their original homeland.
15 Z. Bauman, *Postmodern Ethics*, Oxford: Blackwell, 1993, p. 240.

Neo-tribes, or gangs or clans are the response to the experience of being out of place and existentially homeless. In such a fragmented context there is little purpose in being 'counter-cultural', because in a fragmented, neo-tribal world there are a multitude of alternative lifestyles – and plenty who want to be part of the 'resistance'.

Decadence is a powerful label that describes hopelessness in the midst of plenty. Decadence implies a lack of moral and intellectual discipline that brings neglect or disparagement of moral traditions. Decadent societies are often prosperous but unequal. Those with resources become complacent and never satisfied with what they have, whilst those without wealth become alienated or apathetic. History and literature often focus on the poor or bizarre leadership of decadent societies, because a symptom of decadence is unwillingness to shoulder responsibility. The French postmodernists such as De Certeau, the infamous Derrida and Foucault focus on how bewitched people have become by retailing, entertainment, eroticism and addictions and this feeds a rampant, decadent individualism of 'I am, I want and I will.' Furthermore, the very appetite to resist has been dulled by this daily fodder and as a result, postmodern and globalising societies are not just fragmented but profoundly atomised, and denuded of values that encourage sustained attentiveness to the needs of the other.

Such dismal assessment of the inability and indifference towards anything other than personal pleasure is summarised by Neil Postman in his book *Amusing Ourselves to Death*, describing how we are captivated by watching rather than participating in civil society. The denouement of this preoccupation with pleasure seeking is that it deadens the inclination and wherewithal to solve social decay and pressing environmental problems – and we all know it. Once again the dystopian downward spiral culminates in a loss of confidence in the capacity to do anything different. The events in our world both generate fear and add to a sense that nothing can be trusted. So that even when warnings are given, the wherewithal to do anything about it has deserted us. No wonder we are bothered and bewildered.

Whilst the dense prose of postmodern commentators might be off-putting, art can provide a more immediate expression of our dystopian mood. Whilst analysis is always behind the pace, artists can be the prophets; although unlike Old Testament prophets they have no compunction to embrace a struggle to keep hope alive. Artists such as Damien Hirst, Tracy Emin and Francis Bacon, as well as many others, refuse to offer comfort or reassurance, and insist on confronting the onlooker with savage bleakness and the futility represented by fervent hedonism. We are invited to drink from more and more bitter sources, as we contemplate a dystopian future with the loss of possibility of purposeful action being able to make the world a better place.

DON'T TRUST RELIGION

In a deeply dystopian context, ideas of personal and societal transformation risk naivety and romanticism rather than realism. Furthermore, making a case for the Christian faith as a driver for hopeful and purposeful action is even less likely to be convincing. The idea that Christians can help the world to change for the better sounds increasingly ludicrous. Whilst Christians might have confidence in the transformational capacity of the Christian faith, few others do. In fact, more and more seem inclined to think just the opposite: that those who see their faith as a force for good in the world are not just plain deluded, they are dangerously deluded. As the T-shirts and the fridge magnets say, 'Religion Kills'.

At a more intellectually respectable level, Samuel P. Huntington's analysis[16] has promoted this idea of religion as a source of division and distress, and it is an analysis that has become popular with policy-makers and the media. Huntington's thesis outlines a future where the great divisions among humankind and the dominating source of conflict are cultural, and the likely clash is prompted by the competing religions of Christianity and Islam. The coordinated suicide attacks by al-Qaeda on the United States on 11 September 2001 have served to strengthen the validity of Huntington's analysis.

Huntington justifies his assessment that Christianity (upon which Western civilisation is based) and Islam are likely sources of conflict because both are:

- missionary religions, seeking conversion of others;

---

16   Samuel P. Huntington, *The Clash of Civilizations and the Remaking of World Order*, New York: Simon & Schuster, 1996.

- universal, 'all-or-nothing' religions, in the sense that both sides believe that only their faith is the correct one;
- teleological religions, whose values and beliefs represent the goals and purpose of human existence.

Oliver McTernan confirms this alarming assessment: 'The competing claims on the exclusivity or superiority of one interpretation of one truth over the other have often led to abandonment or outright violation of these [connecting] principles.'[17] The challenge that purposeful, committed Christians face (and likewise purposeful, committed Moslems) is to acknowledge that 'There is a particular danger in religion ... For all religions claim to mediate the absolute. It is easy to topple over the brink and identify that absolute with the finite and fallible human structures through which that absolute is disclosed to human beings.'[18] Keith Ward observes, 'There is brutal, callous, intolerant religion and there is compassionate, kind and tolerant religion.'[19] However, this observation that religion, and Christianity and Islam in particular, can be 'both and' is mostly ignored in a fragmented and intellectually sluggish society.

This contrast between the way Christians perceive our actual and potential contribution to the flourishing of society, compared with how formal religion is viewed by those who have no faith or prefer to be 'spiritual', means that increasingly religion gets blamed for our unhappy dismal state of affairs. Unsurprisingly, this has led to growing numbers who welcome the decline in support for formal Christianity, hoping it will continue and lead to the definitive liquidation of formal or institutional religion. This would, for them, bring about a reduction in their fears for the future. Furthermore, there is greater permission to voice this desire. Christians, for the first time since before Christendom, now experience a public case being made for the suppression of the Christian faith, as well as other faiths, in relation to the public domain.

---

17 O. McTernan, *Violence in God's Name*, New York: Orbis, 2003, p. 148.
18 R. Harries, *God Outside the Box*, London: SPCK, 2002, p. 78.
19 K. Ward, *What the Bible Really Teaches*, London: SPCK, 2004, p. 121.

NO TRUSTING GOVERNMENTS AND STATE

An assumption has grown that 'the government' carries the responsibility for making our world a better place, and then blaming 'the government' when it fails to deliver. This is one of the decadent habits in our society because the public domain is everyone's responsibility: that is the essence of the *polis* – a body of citizens. However, the public domain has lost credibility. Even democracy, in the fragmented environment of globalising nations, fails to build social cohesion. As is now often the case, the *majority* of people are 'middling' in terms of resources, but increasingly insecure and without the moral stretch to put the needs of others above their own, and therefore voting ceases to be an integrative force. Rather, it becomes the very opposite: it becomes a driver that widens the gap between richer and poorer, as the interests of the poor, although numerically significant, cannot match the political clout of the 'middling majority. This can in turn trigger a further nasty process, because when the gap between the rich and the poor gets wider, everyone experiences a loss of well-being, including the rich. This is the finding made by Richard Wilkinson,[20] an epidemiologist and specialist in public health. His extensive cross-cultural research highlights the deep cost of the growing gap between rich and poor across the globe. Wilkinson's research identifies the mutuality and interconnectedness of our interests and well-being, and suggests that when things are grim the inclination is to become protective and defensive rather than attentive and generous in relation to the needs of others.

In the anxious atmosphere of dismal times, generosity of spirit shrinks and the primitive inclination to pursue self-interest increasingly dominates. In our dystopian times, an expression of mutuality that risks unravelling is the obligation of younger generations to attend to the needs of older generations. *Intergenerational equity* is a movement to promote the interests of younger and future generations in the political process, and it does this by questioning the assumption that each working generation will

---

20 See R.G. Wilkinson, *The Impact of Inequality: How to Make Sick Societies Healthier*, London: Routledge, 2005.

take care of the one that preceded it. As the populations of 'advanced' nations become increasingly aged, the elderly population grows bigger and becomes richer and makes more demands on public services. This coincides with a loss of 'assets' by the younger generations who face very high housing costs, minimal pensions and loss of job security. Add to this the temptation for younger people to hold older generations responsible for wrecking the planet and the case for the prosecution becomes a strong one; the jury is already out.

Bureaucracy has grown and grown as more and more government policies need to be implemented. However, bureaucracy tends to disappoint, frustrate and intrude rather than bring efficiency, order and fairness. Max Weber foresaw this expansion of bureaucratic structures to more and more aspects of life. He anticipated that bureaucracy would become like an *iron cage*, restricting, or even forbidding spontaneous and humane behaviour. Weber also anticipated that this would bring a clash of *legitimate* interests – from which the least powerful come out worst. As bureaucracy becomes more and more complex, those who supervise the bureaucratic system gain a healthy living, but the proportion of money that reaches the poor decreases as the bureaucracy requires more and more secure, living-wage administrative jobs to keep it running. This has led to the insult 'poverty pimp' to describe those who make a healthy living on the 'backs of the poor'. However, this is not something that is new: Jeremiah was a millennium-and-a-half ahead of Weber in recognising this dynamic, and he did not mince his words about this *inevitable* feature of human organisation:

> Among my people are wicked men who lie in wait like men who snare birds ... set traps to catch men. Their houses are full of deceit; they have become rich and powerful and have grown fat and sleek. Their evil deeds have no limits; they do not plead the case of the fatherless to win it, they do not defend the rights of the poor.[21]

---

21   Jeremiah 5:26–28.

NOTHING CAN BE DONE

The idea of *inevitability* is an important aspect of a dystopian perspective because it expresses not just things going wrong, but a loss of confidence in the ability of homo sapiens to deal with the world. So there are two things going on in dystopian thinking. The first involves the ever-lengthening list of things going awry. So in addition to all that I have already mentioned, I could have focused on the growth of indebtedness, environmental degradation, the inequities of world trade, the development of drug-resistant disease, international terrorism and ever-increasing 'security', water shortages, bird flu and HIV/AIDS, warfare and ... the list could go on. However, the second aspect of dystopian thinking moves us even closer to hopelessness, that humankind does not have the wherewithal to find a way through the mounting chaos and that there is a predictability about the future being worse than the past.

The recognition of the *persistence* of human frailty is new and it increases the relevance of the Christian faith. When human frailty is acknowledged as not just an occasional blip but an enduring state, we become more aware of our need to be saved. The salvation that Jesus brings becomes more and more relevant, although the offer of salvation that Jesus brings still faces the difficulty of its implausibility – basically it remains hard to believe. However, there is another aspect of salvation that Jesus offers which is not so implausible. An essential aspect of a dystopian outlook is that we need to be *saved from ourselves*, and it is in relation to this that the *fact* that Jesus lived on earth carries salvation. This growing recognition that we need to be saved from ourselves puts the life of Jesus in the focus. The salvation that Jesus brings is not limited to saving us from our sinfulness because he died for us as a propitiation for our sins. It is the fact of his incarnation that provides us with vital clues about how to live.

Mission, as expressed through *fresh expressions* and *mission-shaped church* is inclined to major on the message of good news of reassurance that our persistent frailty and inability to do good is not the final word because Jesus has made us right with God. But there is also the pastoral task of 'saving us from ourselves', i.e. helping people to explore how to live when informed by the pointers that Jesus gives from his life and teaching. When people are bothered and bewildered mission and pastoral care need to be closely interwoven, because when they work together it becomes possible not just to proclaim hope but to enact hope. Elaine Graham, commenting on the role of pastoral care in a time of uncertainty notes that pastoral care has the capacity to disclose 'the core values of the Christian faith, and situate the truth-claims of the (Christian) community in its purposeful enactment, believing also that such sacraments of human agency will elicit signs of transcendence'.[22]

The aim of what follows is not to analyse the factors contributing to the growing dystopian mood, but rather to map potential responses, especially responses that Christians can make, and responses that the institutional churches can make, as we fumble for a response to the new situations that confront humankind. What is clear is that any *talk* of hope by Christians is likely to be unconvincing and to sound cheap in the context of so much dismay. However, as Christians we cannot and must not give up on hope. In a dystopian world, hope, if it is to be believable, has to be enacted. In fact this has always been the case, but now, when the world is worried rather than optimistic, the responsibility for keeping hope alive has become both lonely and urgent.

---

22 E. Graham, *Transforming Practice: Pastoral Theology in an Age of Uncertainty*, Oregon: Wipf and Stock, 2002, p. 210 (previously published by Mowbray, 1996).

2 Silence at Mission Control

Apollo 13 to Mission Control: 'Huston we have a problem ... There's one whole side of the spacecraft missing.' Jim Lovell conveyed this stark reality to Mission Control as the Apollo 13 astronauts got their first view of the damage caused by an explosion. Shortly after, Jim Lovell says to Mission Control: 'Let's look at this from the position of status. What do we have on the space craft that actually works?' This was followed by silence at Mission Control.

This chilling reprise of the fraught conversations between the astronauts and Mission Control is an epic. Apollo 13 was to be the third lunar landing attempt, but the mission was aborted after the rupture of the service module's oxygen tank. After rigorous evaluation, the mission was classed as a 'successful failure'. The mission clearly failed in relation to its objectives, but the crew returned safely to earth despite the odds stacked against them. The success was that the training, expertise, character and commitment of those in Mission Control and the astronauts themselves proved adequate in the face of impending disaster. The story of Apollo 13 is both encouraging and alarming, and it is a story that is fitting for our dismal times.

When the context is dystopian, Christians, like everyone else and like the crew of Apollo 13, have to make friends with the expectation that things will get worse, maybe much worse, and to hold open the possibility that things might never get better. Times like these challenge Christians to ponder what we mean by hope. Having concentrated efforts on understanding and responding to postmodernity, the task is to figure out how, with this shift from upbeat to downbeat mood, Christians have to learn anew what our hope consists of, and what we might have to offer the world. This is not just an academic or theoretical task, because dystopia, in denying the possibility of hope, becomes an anti-Christ. It destroys the hope that Jesus brings to the world, and for this reason the loss of hope associated with a dystopian worldview has to be fought against. However, people cannot be argued out of a dystopian mood, if hope is to be conveyed it is not sufficient for it just to be conveyed by words.

INFORMING OR PERFORMING?

In times of dismay it is not sufficient for Christians to rest in the comforting words of Paul to the Thessalonians that we should not 'grieve as others do who have no hope' (*1 Th* 4:13). This gift that the unknowable future is enfolded in assurance makes it possible to live creatively and generously in the present, and it is essential that this assurance is never separated from the challenge of living creatively and generously. A commitment to discipleship means we cannot allow ourselves assurance without translating this into a distinctive, day-to-day 'performance'. Pope Benedict XVI says this very elegantly in his Encyclical Letter, 'Spe Salvi:'

> The Christian message was not only 'informative' but 'performative'. That means: the Gospel is not merely a communication of things that can be known – it is one that makes things happen and is life-changing. The dark door of time, of the future, has been thrown open. The one who has hope lives differently; the one who hopes has been granted the gift of a new life.[1]

Christians are called not just to have hope but to perform or enact hope, here and now. The Good News is not just a communication, it also makes things happen. This puts a clear challenge at the heart of discipleship: how is hope to be construed and performed? And more precisely: what is a realistic way of construing hope when confidence in progress has plummeted, and when one-time optimism has been superseded by worries about human, technological and environmental malfunctions? One way of responding to dismal times is to relegate hope to 'end times' so that that 'End of the World' scenarios and an impending apocalypse become

---

1   'Spe Salvi', Encyclical Letter of Pope Benedict XIV, Libreria Editrice Vaticana, 2007, para 4.

welcome. However, to make hope consequential on the end of the world, and therefore reduce discipleship to waiting and even longing for such an event, falls prey to two critiques. The first comes from Jesus, who warned about the wastefulness of living life waiting for the thief who might come in the night.

The second critique makes such longing a candidate for being *the* sin against the Holy Spirit. William Bouwsma suggests that commitment to struggle is an essential element of Christian maturity. He also suggests that the worst state of humankind is not our sinfulness, because a central tenet of our faith is that sins can be forgiven – rather, it is the avoidance of or quitting from 'struggle' – because to quit from struggle is to reject or deny the creation process in which God calls us to participate.[2] For these two powerful reasons it is as well to put 'end of the world' hypotheses to the back of one's mind.

NO HOPE FOR YOU

Christians, like everyone else, are not immune to anxiety, and like everyone else, the main temptation, when confronted by dismal times, is to withdraw from the world and become preoccupied with personal and household well-being. For Christians such an 'I'm alright Jack' mentality carries echoes of the heresy of gnosticism. I use the term gnosticism at risk of turning off non-technical readers, but gnosticism is not a complicated notion. In the history of the church, gnosticism was judged a heresy because gnostics were preoccupied with gaining personal insights which brought personal salvation at the expense of a commitment to a world made new, i.e. personal 'safety' and reassurance that they are all right with God, because the world is essentially a bad place to be. Martin Buber, the great Jewish philosopher, considered that the perpetual enemy of faith in the true God is not atheism (the claim that there is no God), but rather gnosticism, with its claim to know the mind of God.

Buber suggested that it is a mistake to view gnosticism as a historical movement; rather, it is a faulty form of religion that will

---

2   W. Bouwsma, 'Christian Adulthood', in E. Erikson (ed.), *Adulthood*, New York: Norton, 1976.

always be with us.[3] Gnosticism is a constant temptation because of the human inclination to claim personal knowledge of God's revelation. The gnostic, both historically and as an ever-present threat today, views the world as dystopian. The desire of the gnostic, therefore, is to forgo this nasty world in order to be close to God. However, if God is good but the world is bad, there must be a separation between heaven (where God is) and earth.

> The cardinal feature of Gnostic thought is the radical dualism that governs the relation of God and world, and correspondingly that of man and world. The deity is absolutely transmundane,[4] its nature alien to that of the universe which it neither created nor governs and to which it is the complete antithesis ... the world is the work of lowly powers.[5]

Categorising the world as dystopian, i.e. devoid of hope, is full of hazards for Christians. Not least because there are plenty of Bible-based urgings why Christians cannot embrace a dystopian, or hopeless view of the world, basically because the world has been created by God – and God considers it to be good:[6]

- God's creation was good ... 'In the beginning God created the heavens and the earth. ... God saw all that he had made, and it was very good.'[7]
- In the New Testament it is clear that the 'Word' (Jesus) is co-creator with God the Father. 'He was with God in the beginning. Through him all things were made; without him nothing was made that has been made.'[8]

---

3   See M. Buber, *The Eclipse of God*, trans Stanley Godman, New York: Harper and Bros, 1952, p. 175.
4   Transmundane means beyond the world or worldly matters.
5   H. Jonas, *The Gnostic Religion*, Boston: Beacon Press, 1963, p. 42.
6   I am indebted to conversations with Mark Perrott on the impact of Gnosticism on evangelicalism today and in particular I am indebted to his work 'In the City, But Not Of It' submitted for MTh in Christian Doctrine (2005); Spurgeon's College, University of Wales for these references.
7   Genesis 1:31 NIV.
8   John 1:2–3 NIV.

- In Ephesians, the writer articulates God's plan 'to make plain to everyone the administration of this mystery, which for ages past was kept hidden in God, who created all things'.[9]
- Again, in Colossians, 'For by him all things were created: things in heaven and on earth, visible and invisible, whether thrones or powers or rulers or authorities; all things were created by him and for him.'[10]

A CELTIC CORRECTIVE

If Christians are to retain a commitment to 'a world made new', rather than drift into selfish, dystopian gnosticism, it is essential that the relationship between heaven and earth is nuanced, rather than separated as heaven and eternity 'good' and all that is earthly 'bad'. Such nuancing is a characteristic of Celtic Christianity. In contrast to gnosticism, Celtic Christianity continually celebrated the interwoven relationship between earth and heaven, resulting in rejoicing in the tiny miracles of nature and the blessing of mundane items that support daily living. The symbols associated with Celtic spirituality emphasise how heaven (or eternity) and this world are woven together. For example, the familiar Celtic knot is a symbol of a unified whole that has neither beginning nor end.

Following the proclamation in the Letter to the Hebrews 'Since we are surrounded by so great a cloud of witnesses',[11] Celtic spirituality rejoices in the accompaniment in this life by saints who have gone ahead of us. This inspired the Welsh poet Waldo Williams to write that we are 'keeping house in a cloud of witnesses',[12] thus linking daily life with eternity. When the Godly eternal gets so interwoven with everyday life it is impossible to smother hope.

Celtic Christianity has experienced a renewal in recent times, particularly by the Iona Community. George MacLeod, the founder of the Iona Community described Iona as a 'thin place', where only a tissue separated heaven and earth and the awareness of God. The pattern of commitment expressed by the now international Iona

---

9   Ephesians 3:9 NIV.
10 Colossians 1:16 NIV.
11 Hebrews 12:1 NIV.
12 From W. Williams, 'Peacemaker', trans. Tony Conran, in *What is Man?*, Landysul: Gomer Press, 1997, p. 131

Community, speaks of how it is possible to embrace, rather than escape from, the struggles of life, whilst holding firm to the ancient confidence 'that all shall be well'. The Iona Community describes itself as 'A dispersed Christian ecumenical community working for peace and social justice, rebuilding of community and the renewal of worship'.[13] This represents an engaged rather than an escapist vision, and well it should, because human beings are, by the grace of God, co-creators of the earth.

In our 'outrageous pursuit of hope' (to use a phrase from Mary C. Grey[14]), Christians confronted by dystopian perspectives can no longer just *proclaim* or assert the persistence of hope; rather, if confidence in hope is to grow, then hope has to be *demonstrated*, there has to be something that signifies and gives confidence to the reality and possibility of hope. In holding fast to our confidence in hope, the danger is that Christians ignore or downplay the sense that people have of being 'in over our heads', and downplay the extensive perception of how chaos threatens. The hope that Christians need to communicate has to be able to flourish amidst the chill of anxiety and fear that is generated in dismal times. Hope that sidesteps gloom and bleakness is cheap hope; it is an offering that is unworthy of its name. If hope is to be kept alive in the context of dystopia then hope has to be performed, and the tiny, 'bit-by-bit' elements of the practices that make for hope have to be identified, articulated and practised again and again as we fumble for a response to the new situations that confront humankind. No longer can Christians just preach and teach hope, we have to *do* hope.

THE J-CURVE

The J-Curve is a graph used by economists and political scientists. It is a model that is germane to the challenge we face as Christians as we try to re-cast our priorities and practice to take account of how bothered and bewildered our world has become. There are

---

13   See <http://www.iona.org.uk>.
14   M.C. Grey, *The Outrageous Pursuit of Hope*, London: Darton, Longman and Todd, 2000.

two things to note about the J-Curve (or hockey-stick curve as it is sometimes called) that make it particularly relevant:

1   The graph highlights that often there is a period of dangerous instability before positive development can take off and gain momentum.[15] In other words, things can get very tough indeed, but hopeful transformation always remains a possibility, and the darkest hour may prove to be the hour before dawn.
2   Rather than work through the dangerous and distressing period of instability – that's the dip in the curve – courage and resilience might fail, and in response, old habits and practices are restored, sometimes with even more intensity than before.

An example of a J-Curve analysis is provided by the political analyst, Ian Bremmer. He uses the J-Curve to predict the stability of nation states. He suggests that some nation states are stable because they are *closed* to influences from the outside world, whilst others are stable for the opposite reason: they are *open* to public debate and insights and the movement of people and ideas from other parts of the world.

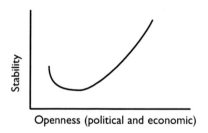

Figure 2.1[16]
Source: Bremmer, p. 6

---

15   In political science, the 'J-Curve' is part of a model developed by James Chowning Davies to explain political revolutions. Davies asserts that revolutions are a subjective response to a sudden reversal in fortunes after a long period of economic growth. The theory is often applied to explain social unrest and efforts by governments to contain this unrest – from Wikipedia 'J-Curve' <http://en.wikipedia.org/wiki/J_curve>.
16   I. Bremmer, *The J-Curve: A New Way to Understand Why Nations Rise and Fall*, New York, Simon and Schuster, 2006.

As Figure 2.1 shows, in a J-Curve, the right side of the curve is higher than the left side, and Bremmer uses the graph to make the case that openness brings a more sustainable, stable society than can be achieved by authoritarian regimes. His case is that authoritarian regimes can also achieve stability, but their very techniques (e.g. control of media, restricting movement in and out of the country) limit the degree of growth the nation can hope for. The point of drawing on Bremmer's analysis is not to debate open societies versus authoritarian regimes, rather it is to highlight the struggle that is necessary in moving from one to the other. Bremmer observes that to develop into an *open* and stable country, a country has to go through a transitional period of dangerous instability. Bremmer cites South Africa as a survivor of that journey, whilst others such as Yugoslavia collapsed.[17] So a J-Curve analysis, as Bremmer suggests, provides a warning: the downward slope and dip in the J-Curve have to be extremely carefully anticipated and negotiated because a totalitarian infrastructure cannot be replaced easily with a more open form of government because that risks inducing chaos and shock.[18] According to Bremmer, once a country has destabilised and fallen from the top left side of the graph into the low pit of instability, it has a choice to make. Will it continue on the route towards openness and the long-term gains of openness and stability? Or will its courage fail? Will the nation, in the moment of chaos, about-face and quickly run back up the left side of the J-Curve?

Richard Beck provides an illustration that resonates more with church life. He uses the J-Curve graph to map the complex dance between the church and the world, and suggests that when a church begins to embrace a more outward looking focus, in all likelihood it will experience a fall in mission effectiveness and may be tempted to abandon the idea, scooting back to its old ways, i.e. back up the short left side of the J-Curve. Beck suggests that if the church is courageous and persists with its new commitment to outward-focused ministry, then this dip will be followed by a rise

---

17 Ibid., p. 5.
18 Bremmer suggests that for this reason any interference in the state of Iraq must be undertaken extremely cautiously if the nation is not to implode. History will prove his prediction to have been correct.

that is greater and more sustained than the fall.[19] In our dystopian context it is possible to anticipate what 'scooting back up the left side of the J-Curve' might look like. It too would involve rejecting the world, and the offer of salvation would be reduced to salvation at the expense of koinonia, i.e. personal assurance at the expense of expressing generosity and goodness towards the wider world.

If our courage fails in the face of chaos and dismay, then the likelihood is that our Christian practice becomes escapist, and we embrace a neo-gnosticism and, like Peter, deny that we know Jesus. If we know anything at all about Jesus we know there can be no scooting back into the safe assurance of personal salvation when the going gets tough, because in following Jesus we are in relationship with the one who gave himself as a ransom for all.[20] In following Jesus we are drawn into his 'being for all'; it is this that shapes our performance, and characterises our way of living. In following Jesus we commit ourselves to live for others: 'Christ died for all, that those who live might live no longer for themselves but for him who for their sake died.'[21] Therefore to live for him means allowing oneself to be drawn into his *being for others*. With this in mind we return to the J-Curve.

The J-Curve graph is used to alert people to the need to attend to the 'dip' sensitively, creatively and courageously. The graph also permits the axes to be labelled on the basis of one's own preference – including one's prejudice. Matt Thurstone, a Mormon commentator, also uses a J-Curve analysis, but in this instance speculates that the decline in mainstream liberal churches, that have embraced women and homosexuals in their leadership, is indicative of the danger that besets inclusive churches. He uses the J-Curve to support his view that liberal, inclusive churches are so fraught with danger that they are destined to move downwards into decline.[22] The J-Curve is open to any hypotheses, and this is both its strength and its weakness. However, this allows the impact of particular variables to be unfurled for consideration and debate, providing a platform on which the case for a whole range of factors can be proposed as

---

19   See the website Experimental Theology <http://experimentaltheology. blogspot.com/2007/02/j-curve-and-missional-church.html>.

20   1 Tim 2:6 NIV.

21   2 Cor 5:15 NIV.

22   See <http://sunstoneblog.com/2006/11/09/the-j-curve/>.

essential ingredients that will bring sustainable health and well-being. With this in mind it is important that I am open about my reason for using the J-Curve in the context of bother and bewilderment. For my purposes, the J-Curve enables certain ideas to be explored:

- In dismal, postmodern times, hope, if it is to be seen and experienced as realistic, cannot just be proclaimed or asserted. In order to be convincing and to generate 'hope', micro-actions are needed that enable hope to be enacted and therefore made real.
- In dismal postmodern times, reflecting on and learning from the way Jesus lived his life will enable our Christian faith to contribute positively to the avoidance of hazards that are dogging our individual and communal lives.

Underlying these ideas a deep commitment to the practice of 'action and reflection' is needed in order to cope with and get beyond the prevailing troubled and tricky times. To promote this deep commitment amongst the growing number who are bothered and bewildered, the process of church needs:

- greater commitment to reflective practice and less emphasis on formulaic expressions of faith;
- greater attention to the micro-actions that demonstrate the viability of earthed or enacted hope and less reliance on asserted or proclaimed hope;
- greater collaboration between the mission task and the practice of pastoral care in order that this resource of 'action and reflection' can be promoted effectively.

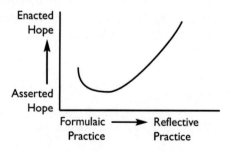

Figure 2.2

If through our process of church we can develop and promote greater reflectiveness rather than promoting faith formulas, then the potential for enacting hope increases significantly, but only if we have the courage to live with the turbulence that will be experienced at the outset. This is to heed the lessons of the J-Curve, that shifting from traditional practice, in this case loosening the emphasis on the formulas of our faith, may bring an initial reduction in the capacity to 'enact hope', i.e. to 'do' or deliver hope. This is because the loosening of well-entrenched orthodoxies will cause upset and disruption, including mockery by the media and bringing a swagger to those who champion atheism.

The culmination of commitment to reflective practice and to enacted or performed hope results in an outcome similar to the pastoral cycle, with its emphasis on a cycle of action and reflection. This is not a new resource for the church, but it is not used very widely. Possibly this is because of the dominance of creedal statements and doctrine that shape our current process of church. Add to this the inclination to assert or simply proclaim hope, a habit that has relied on the fact that, until now, talk of hope has been straightforward in a culture which has been entranced by the continuous, apparently hope-filled developments that have come on the back of scientific and technological advances. This cheap hope has had the effect of stultifying action – or praxis as it is called in the context of 'action and reflection'.

In dystopian times, Christians may find it lonely holding on to hopefulness and the first challenge is to face up to and respond to this. However, there is a second, evangelistic challenge, and that is to help kindle confidence in hope amidst the bothered and bewildered world. It is in this wider context that the resource of 'action and reflection', informed by the way in which Jesus lived, becomes vital. Jesus lived so that the world might have life in all its fullness, and it is this that must bring an exceptional urgency to the mission of the church.

WHAT IS WRONG WITH FORMULAIC FAITH?

My contention is that if our church practice continues with the current emphasis on reciting and preaching the formulas of our faith, and considers it sufficient only to assert or speak of hope, then the offer of salvation made through the process of church will be neither earthed nor convincing. Although the formulas of our Christian faith have been hard won, they are unconvincing to bothered and bewildered people because they are self-referential and self-validating. In a postmodern world the authority of formularies, regardless of who proposes them, has withered. Rather than bring confidence, the formularies of our faith that have been honed over centuries, in a troubled, postmodern world, only serve to confirm the clannishness of the church process, where people speak in riddles that are understandable and *plausible* to only a few.

A further reason why an emphasis on the doctrinal aspect of faith no longer provides a viable platform from which to inspire hopefulness, is that the well-used expressions associated with the formularies of our faith are now cliché-ridden. Just a few examples will suffice: 'Our hands are God's hands in the world' has become a cliché, and another: 'Jesus is Lord' or 'Witnessing to the love of God'. It may be shocking to have these key components of Christian communication and teaching referred to as clichés, but in terms of their ability to convey workaday hope they have neither an impact, nor convey clarity. The problem with the clichés that pepper our efforts to proclaim hope, is not just failure of the imagination in relation to our terminology – there is something more serious. The way we have repeatedly construed hope for our world has become trapped in *'thought-terminating* clichés'. A thought-terminating cliché deals with an issue by providing an answer that is impossible to question, serving to end the discussion, cutting off further questions and interrupting the flow of thought.

The power of thought-terminating clichés is illustrated in a story told by S. Yizhar, the Israeli novelist. He tells the story of young soldiers clearing the inhabitants out of an apparently peaceful Arab village during Israel's War of Independence. Following orders, they take control of the village, killing and wounding some of the villagers, but mostly loading into trucks the women, children and old people they have rounded up. One truck driver wonders why they aren't allowed any belongings or water?

'There is no stuff,' the soldiers tell him, angry at being forced to voice this appalling detail.

'There's nothing. Take them away from here and let them go to hell.' The soldiers tell each other that these villagers are 'like animals'.

Then, one of the soldiers voices a moral qualm, 'Are we killing them?'

'We're taking them to their side. It is very decent of us ...'

'What will happen to them there?'
'Let them ask their ... leaders'.
'What will they eat or drink?'
'They should have thought of that before they started all this.'
'Started what?' asks the young soldier.
'Stop thinking so much!' shouts his colleague.[23]

Thought-terminating clichés are widespread and clearly it is not just Christians who have tumbled over this tripwire.[24] Wikipedia provides a long list, citing familiar expressions such as 'There's no silver bullet'; 'Such is life'; 'God has a plan and a purpose'; and from a more politically charged realm: 'Support our troops'; 'This is for security reasons'; '... or the terrorists win'; 'My body, my choice'; 'Better dead than Red!' Such clichés are not just signs of lazy thinking, they have, according to Robert Jay Lifton, more sinister consequences. Lifton was the first to use the term 'thought-terminating cliches' in his book 'Thought Reform and the Psychology of Totalism'. From his research he observed that

> The group develops a jargon unique to itself, often non-understandable to outsiders. This jargon consists of numerous words and phrases which the members understand (or think they understand), but which really act to dull one's ability to engage in critical thinking. It is actually made up of thought-terminating clichés. The most far-reaching and complex of human problems are compressed into brief, definitive-sounding phrases, easily memorized and easily expressed. Thought-provoking complexities are bypassed and ultimate truth is expressed in a single phrase or even a word.[25]

---

23   This conversation is taken from *Khirbet Khizeh* by S. Yizhar published by Ibis and reviewed by Ruth Padel in *Prospect*, June 2008.

24   Chris Hedges uses the phrase, 'thought-terminating cliché' to describe the way our society has learned to function, which is anti-thought and anti-self-reflection. See Chris Hedges interview in 'Oldspeak' the online journal of the Rutherford Institute, 6 February 2008; see <http://www.rutherford.org/oldspeak/Articles/Interviews>.

25   The two quotations in this paragraph are slightly adapted from R.J. Lifton, *Thought Reform and the Psychology of Totalism*, North Carolina: University of North Carolina Press, repr. 1989, p. 429.

Lifton argues from his research into brainwashing that, in 'totalist' environments, the 'thought-terminating cliché' becomes the start and finish of any ideological analysis.[26] If our church process persists in putting doctrine and thought-terminating clichés that reduce the possibility for dialogue to the fore, this carries an immense cost at a time when people are searching for 'truth-tellers' and honest thinkers. So this is serious. Unless we can move beyond 'thought-terminating clichés' and doctrine honed in academe as a means of sharing the hope that is at the heart of the Gospels, we risk falling prey to a new version of gnosticism. By persisting with the formulas of our faith, that are meaningful to those who have been formed in the faith, but which are inscrutable or alienating to others, we fail to deliver the inclusive grace or generosity that is the motivating energy at the heart of God's love for his creation.

We face a deeply challenging conundrum. The teaching that Christians derive from the Bible and tradition necessitates that we never give up on articulating the persistence and reality of earthly hope – a 'this world' hope which can never be overcome. However, in dystopian, postmodern times, it is unrealistic to represent hope on the basis of doctrine or teaching. Whilst for the adept or 'formed' Christian it may be viable to engender hopefulness by reference to verses from the Bible, or by erudition in relation to the Kingdom of God, such methods can no longer cross the ever-thickening membrane between believer and non-believer, or half-believer, who make up the bulk of the population. Whilst Christians might gain reassurance about the enduring nature of hope from biblical passages, few others are reassured by such a self-referential process.

It is for these reasons that reliance on the established and well-honed formularies of the Christian faith is unlikely to advance the cause of enacted or earthed hope. But there are other reasons. Formulaic faith is essentially bossy. It requires someone, or an institution, to tell others what to think. It assumes one party in the relationship knows better than the other. Formulaic faith implies control, and this assumes one party is not 'in over their heads', but secure in their competence to deal with most if not all eventualities. Furthermore, when the control that is associated with formulaic faith combines with unaccountability, this develops into the unholy

---

26   Ibid.

force of totalitarianism, a position that does not permit alternatives. Historically, the churches in Europe achieved a near-totalitarian environment, sometimes by using violence to insist that everyone assented to the formularies of the faith. The church has had the power to make rules or doctrine, and to admonish people to prevent them from straying from the specified doctrines of the church. Without effective accountability, control can go beyond bossiness to bullying, where the power of one group to direct another can be exercised brutally, and, more artfully, control can also be exercised subtly.

A faith that is prescribed by established formulas or doctrines requires certain *roles*, and it is the role of clergy in particular in which authority was vested, and to an extent remains vested. The role of the clergyman was territorially focused, and within that domain he had the capacity to affirm or condemn, and so direct the behaviour of the people in that place. In the current shorn state of the churches such a description seems cartoon-like. But even today, churches give lots of energy to ensure that their rules are kept: directing who can be godparents; who can be married – and where; directing what can be blessed – and what is too profane to be blessed; directing who can preach, and what creeds are to be recited. This capacity to sanction and forbid, in today's perspective, is antithetical to transformation. Today, the idea of transformation carries with it the implication of a welcome embrace of particular behaviours rather than being subject to the direction of others.

Emboldened by the Enlightenment, people have freed themselves gradually from the church's fearsome teaching about the nature of God, and more and more backed their own hunches about God. Now the state provides people with ways of circumventing the traditional restrictions enforced by the church, and it is the state which legitimises our behaviour rather than the once-powerful church. Today, no agency finds it easy to *tell* people what to think, although there are clearly more subtle ways of persuasion; otherwise the marketing industry would have declined long ago.

THE CASE FOR REFLECTIVENESS

In the J-Curve graph being proposed, the opposite of formulaic practice is reflective practice, and the case is made that in troubled times, by investing in reflective practice, Christians will be better able to move from asserted hope towards enacted hope. The suggestion is that by practising reflectiveness it becomes possible to embark on the upward, sustainable right side of the J-Curve to achieve a resilient, responsive and distinctive unfurling of our Christian faith, with its hopeful and transformational capacity. In addition, this practice of reflectiveness is recommended not just as Christian practice but for bothered and bewildered people in the wider world. Reflectiveness is important because it enables a host of helpful processes and practices in relation to living in a world which is not just postmodern, or post-Christendom, but dystopian.

Reflectiveness might on first consideration seem to consist of a combination of prayerfulness and mulling things over. It is both these things, but it is also a tough and disciplined practice that has a distinctive edge to it. It was Donald Schön,[27] writing in the 1970s, who first identified the 'edge' that makes for deep reflectiveness. He realised that in (the then) modern society, 'change' had become a fundamental feature of life.[28] Today this observation seems routine, but Schön was one of the first commentators to recognise that stability and 'unchangeability' can no longer be taken as the norm, and that people need to be equipped to deal with uncertainty and continuous change. Schön went on to provide further insights – insights that are particularly relevant to a J-Curve analysis.

According to Schön, institutions are characterised by 'dynamic conservatism': 'A tendency to fight to remain the same'.[29] Therefore, institutions as well as individuals have to learn to achieve a reflectiveness, or, to use Schön's terminology, to develop as 'learning systems' that can achieve continued responsiveness to changing circumstances, but also avoid insupportable disruption. Thus, 'dynamic conservatism' is not a negative form of resistance to change, rather, it helps to ensure that change is achieved without an intolerable threat to the essential functions that the system or institution fulfils. Schön comments: 'Our systems need to maintain

---

27 My comments on the work of Donald Schön have been helpfully informed by the work of Mark K. Smith writing on Donald Schön in the Encyclopaedia of Informal Education <http://www.infed.org>.
28 This focus on change and industrial society is expounded in his ground-breaking book, D.A. Schön, *Beyond the Stable State Public and Private Learning in a Changing Society*, Harmondsworth: Penguin, 1973.
29 Ibid, p. 30.

their identity, and their ability to support the self-identity of those who belong to them, but they must at the same time be capable of transforming themselves.'[30] Here is an approach that at least *aims* to respond appropriately and generously to the friability and potentially unhelpful fractiousness that is associated with the dip in the J-Curve.

Reflective practice, by its very nature, is respectful of that which already holds sway, because reflective practice values the ability to 'draw upon certain routines ... to bring fragments of memories into play and begin to build theories and responses that fit the new situation'.[31] *Reflectiveness is not a companion of subversion, nor is reflectiveness about reckless undermining of established practice.* However, reflective practice is always alert to how established, controlling practice cannot but fall short in a continually changing world.

For those trained in youth work and informal education it will come as no surprise that reflectiveness is commended. Youth workers in particular are encouraged to 'think on their feet', consciously drawing on a repertoire of theories and metaphors that shape youth work practice – whilst also remaining alert – and intrigued, rather than threatened, by events and encounters that challenge this repertoire. It is this capacity that makes reflective practice so important in dismal times. Reflective practice is a resource for coping with the scary sense of being 'in over our heads',[32] to coin an expression used by Robert Kegan. It is also a vital skill when coping with the dip in the J-Curve when it becomes necessary to be able to act without having a full understanding of things.

Reflective practice is the meeting place with the Holy Spirit, as it is the process through which discernment is forged, and this makes reflective practice sacramental, in that it is a means of grace. Reflectiveness, and the learning that comes from it, is, as with all sacraments, a means of extending God's grace; it provides a tangible expression of the empowerment given by God to people, so that discipleship can be venturesome, involving exploration, struggle

---

30 Ibid, p. 57.
31 Smith, Encyclopaedia of Informal Education.
32 R. Kegan, *In Over Our Heads: The Mental Demands of Modern Life*, Cambridge, MA: Harvard University Press, 1994.

and ultimately the discovery of deep truth. Mary C. Grey suggests that the 'Holy Spirit leads us to cross and recross boundaries in order to recognise God's action in new and surprising ways'.[33] She suggests that it is 'Through the initiative of the Holy Spirit ... creating new transgressive[34] energies for life, for connection across boundaries'.[35] It is this energy, that enables us to cross the fragmented terrain of a globalising and (neo)tribalistic world, that is so essential if we are to find life-giving rather than death-dealing ways through our dystopian context. It is only by the application of reflectiveness, as a means of fostering the imagination, that it becomes possible to enact hope. The capacity for reflection, alongside love and generosity, provides the threefold dynamic which can gently, but progressively, engage with dismay and the loss of hope.

HOPE FROM WORDS OR HOPE THROUGH ACTION?

In this proposed model of the J-Curve a distinction is made between 'asserted hope' and 'enacted hope'. Asserted hope is a hangover from the power-ridden days of Christendom. Asserted hope relies on traditional authority or fluent rhetoric. It involves one party asserting or declaiming 'In God we trust,' or 'In Jesus there is salvation,' or 'Jesus is Lord.' Asserted hope is not wrong or misleading. The problem is that for more and more people it is unconvincing. Asserted hope in difficult times also carries a risk because it is the tool of fascist leaders; it is the resource drawn on in totalitarian environments. In worrisome times Homo sapiens is prone to be gullible and prone to wish-fulfilment, desirous of protection from those who use their capacity for *asserting* hope as a route to power.

The story of Apollo 13 is a story of enacted hope. Had Mission Control asserted hope, rather than worked with the crew to identify a series of actions, the spacecraft and the lives of the crew would have been lost. Enacted hope is hope that is accompanied by action. Enacted hope is tangible because it involves micro-actions

---

33   Grey, p. 82.
34   Transgressive, meaning passing beyond some limit or crossing a boundary.
35   Grey, p. 79.

which might on first view seem insignificant. Enacted hope is at work in the story of the woman at the well. Her encounter with Jesus is worth scrutiny to help identify how micro-actions contribute to enacted hope.

AND THEN THERE IS CONVERSATION ...

The conversation that Jesus has with the woman who comes to draw water from Jacob's well is also a story of enacted hope. His conversation with the Samaritan woman is the longest recorded conversation that Jesus has with anyone (John 4:7–26). It provides an excellent example of how conversation can enact hope, because conversation involve a series of micro-actions, and in particular, can be open to the transgressive energy that speaks of the Holy Spirit's urge to extend the bonds of love across cultures and communities.[36]

- Jesus was tired and hot and thirsty and without any access to the fresh water (John 4:7, 8).
  First micro-action = a conversation where the supposedly powerful speaks from a position of vulnerability.

- Jesus asks for water from a Samaritan woman (John 4:8, 9).
  Second micro-action = stepping outside the restrictions of tribalism.

- There is friendly banter about water that never runs out, saving all the hard work of drawing the water from a very deep well (John 4:13–15).
  Third micro-action = mutual commitment to sustain the encounter.

- Jesus says 'Go, call your husband and come back' (John 4:16).
  Fourth micro-action = sensitivity on the part of Jesus to the

---

36 Grey reminds us of how in Christian tradition the Holy Spirit is described as *vinculum amoris* – the bond of love, the divine 'glue' uniting and bonding communities across cultures. See Grey, p. 61.

impossibility of sustaining the conversation whilst the woman is by herself. Custom made a sustained conversation by a woman with a male stranger hugely inappropriate and would bring damage to the woman's reputation.

- The woman says 'I have no husband' (John 4:17).
  Fifth micro-action = risk taking: the woman feels confident enough to make a disclosure

- Jesus suddenly understands her situation: how she has been passed from pillar to post (five men have married her and divorced her, and the bloke who has taken her in this time isn't prepared to give her the status of wife). Furthermore, Jesus can now make sense of why she comes to draw water in the heat of the day: she is so excluded and disparaged by her neighbours that she finds it preferable to draw her water in the midday heat when no-one else will be at the well (John 4:18).
  Sixth micro-action = a compassionate 'ah ha',[37] i.e. a sudden insight into how it is for the other person.

- The woman recognises the potency of Jesus and tries to change the direction of the conversation (John 4:19, 20).
  Seventh micro-action = a retreat into tribalism.

- Jesus explains the possibility of a God of truth whom everyone can worship in Spirit (John 4:21–24).
  Eighth micro-action = an offer of a new inclusive paradigm.

- The woman recalls that she knows something about this, and that a Messiah will explain things to us (John 4:25).
  Ninth micro-action = personal experience and knowledge coalesce.

---

37 The assumption that Jesus rebukes the woman at the well because she is a 'loose' woman, is to project the church's longstanding preoccupation with sexual misdemeanour onto this exceptional encounter. Knowledge of the mores of the time make it clear that this would have been a deeply vulnerable and possibly bruised and battered woman, with no choice other than to be reliant on a man to give her food and shelter. In return she would have helped in the house, maybe warmed his bed and would likely have been treated with distain by others in the household.

- Jesus declares 'I who speak to you am he' and the conversation continues until the disciples return.

- At this point the actions cease to be 'micro', for the woman dashes back to the village to encourage people to come out to the well where she has met up with a man who could be the Christ. (John 4:26–30).

It becomes clear that the encounter was as deeply significant for Jesus as it was for the woman (John 4:31–38). The people of the village asked Jesus to stay with them, and he stayed for two days and they recognised Jesus as the Messiah. This story highlights the potency of conversation, especially when conversation involves people who have been formed by different cultures, as was the case with the woman at the well and Jesus, and as it is increasingly the case in a world of hyper-mobility and fragmentation. Conversations carry risk: not only are opinions, emotions and experiences likely to shared, these details are shared in a context where there can be no guarantee against misinterpretation and misunderstanding. This is particularly the case in a fragmented, utterly diverse world where there are fewer and fewer shared experiences and perspectives that can provide a safe foundation for conversation.

Conversation can be a means for the Holy Spirit, providing a way of connecting across boundaries, providing a medium for life-giving transgressive energies. In a globalising world it is a constant challenge to see every person as someone who is known and loved by God. By embarking on conversation we embrace this challenge and we embark on a courageous, experimental micro-action. Theodor Zeldin'[38] comments that conversation is always an experiment with results that can never be guaranteed, as the conversation between Jesus and the woman at the well illustrates. 'Conversation is, among other things, a mind-reading game and a puzzle.' Zeldin goes on, 'We constantly have to guess why others say what they do. We can never be sure when words will dance with each other, opinions caress, imaginations undress, topics open.'[39]

---

38 T. Zeldin, *Conversation*, London: The Harvill Press, 1989, p. 3.
39 Ibid., p. vii.

Conversation is an essential aspect of reflective practice. Often, until we hear ourselves speak we are unable to recognise and own the insights that we have assembled. Mary Wolfe comments that 'Through conversation we turn around our ideas and experiences with each other ... and we thereby also review those ideas and experiences ... conversation provides us with one way in which either to revisit our experiences or to entertain possibilities of future experiences.'[40] Wolfe[41] goes on to describe conversation as 'social communion', because for a conversation to take place there has to be a commitment to the 'co-operative principle'[42] from those involved. Conversation that 'catches fire ... involves more than sending and receiving information',[43] it requires both commitment and courage, and endeavouring to 'give each other courage'[44] in order for the encounter to be sustained. Conversation across difference, such as the conversations Jesus had with the Syro-Phoenician woman[45] and the Samaritan woman at the well, illustrate the tightrope between encounter, intimacy and potential failure as the meeting in conversation can so easily flounder rather than flow.

Far from being inaction, it is often through conversation that we change the way we view the world and embark on changing the world itself. In risking conversation with those whose perspective and life experience are different from our own, we are trusting that patience and generosity of spirit will be found in the other, as we distil in their presence, what we are 'coming to know'. Through conversation we take a first step towards enacting hope, but this requires the courage to make our thoughts public. The micro-action of opening a conversation represents an act of the imagination, and is a spirited signifier of our shared humanity as we seek

---

40 M. Wolfe, 'Conversation', in L.D. Richardson and M. Wolfe (eds), *Principles and Practice of Informal Education*, Oxford: Routledge Falmer, 2003, p. 130.

41 Ibid.

42 Here Wolfe is quoting H.P. Grice, 'Logic and Conversation', in P. Cole and J.L. Morgan (eds), *Syntax and Semantics*, vol. 3: *Speech Acts*, New York: Academic Press, 1975.

43 Zeldin, p. 3.

44 Ibid., p. 28.

45 The story with slight variations is told in Matthew 15:21–28 and Mark 7:24–30.

to express ideas or feelings in a way that will resonate with others. Conversation is surely holy ground, because through conversation we open ourselves to recognising God's action in new and surprising ways.

To return to the encounter that Jesus had with the Samaritan woman at the well, which was left at the point at which I suggested the actions were no longer 'micro' as the woman ran back to the village to encourage people to come out to the well where she has met up with a man who could be the Christ. This is an aspect of the story that deserves more attention than it often gets, because it is a remarkable example of someone finding their voice and having the courage to seek a hearing. The woman at the well had learned to keep herself to herself; the persistent exclusion by others can often lead to self-exclusion, and also to what Paulo Freire refers to as *muteness*.[46] The likelihood is that this woman, who each day tried to avoid meeting up with people as she came to the well, had lost the ability to *speak for herself*. Exclusion easily leads to an inability or reluctance to speak for oneself and make oneself heard, and this is a deeply dehumanising oppression. The conversation that the woman had with Jesus was transformational, cathartic even, because as a result, the woman both found her voice and her courage.

In seeking to be heard and seeking to gather a receptive audience, the woman moves beyond micro-action to public action – she embarks on a political act (in the broadest sense). Margaret Betz Hull, drawing on the work of Hannah Arendt, explains the significance of finding the courage to claim the right to an audience, 'The ability to speak for oneself and the guarantee of a receptive audience become politically charged realities. By extension … lack of a respectful audience (is) to deny the individual his/her basic humanity and the ability to develop into a "'who'" and to not remain merely a "what".'[47] The woman did command a respectful audience, to the extent of moving others to action, who then went on to ask Jesus to remain with them. This story of Jesus' encounter with the woman at the well does more than illustrate the potency

---

46 P. Freire, *Educacao como Pratica da Liberdade*, Rio de Janeiro: Editoria Civilizacao Brasileira, 1967, p. 69.
47 M. Betz Hull, *The Hidden Philosophy of Hannah Arendt*, London: Routledge, 2002, p. 153.

of micro-actions, it does more than illustrate how those who are excluded can find their voice and command a hearing. The story also shows how a thousand tiny empowerments (to coin a phrase from Leonie Sandercock[48]) can gain momentum and lead to the enacting of hope, not just for individuals but also for communities.

---

48 L. Sandercock, *Towards Cosmopolis; Planning for Multicultural Cities*, Chichester: John Wiley & Sons, 1998.

3 Down in the Dip

The previous chapter began with the impending disaster facing Apollo 13. In the end disaster was averted. The 'successful failure' was due to the character, expertise and training of all those involved. Disasters can be averted. However, they require a particular prowess. The skills achieved in training by the astronauts had been closely designed. Mostly, they would have been skills that one hoped would never be drawn upon. In dismal times likewise there are skills to be achieved and character to be formed, and this is particularly the case when contemplating the dip in the J-Curve.

A J-Curve graph is essentially hopeful in that it holds out the possibility of positive outcomes that gain momentum. The J-Curve is also relevant because it acknowledges the real possibility of things turning sour, and thus resonates with the prevailing context of dismay and foreboding. The idea that things can get better is essential to the analysis. However, before this can happen things are likely to get worse, maybe much worse.

Bremmer emphasises how the dip in the J-Curve must be extremely carefully anticipated and negotiated if disastrous and destructive chaos is not to result. Formal religion, particularly the established denominations, are already slipping down the left side of the J-Curve as they face up to the loss of knowledge and respect for the formularies of the Christian faith in the general populace. Furthermore, there is a growing number who would be pleased to see institutional religion (not just Christian) move into terminal decline, which combines with a forceful voicing of this desire. It is a new experience for Christians to have to face arguments being made for the suppression of religious, and particularly Christian, commentary on social and ethical issues.

The main challenges that are pushing churches and Christians ever deeper into the dip come from three directions:

- From the fear that, with globalisation, the level of diversity is such that strong (in the sense of proselytising) religious practice and belief may breach the peace. This is an argument associated with Samuel Huntington (referred to earlier) and much favoured by pundits, and, one suspects, by those behind the scenes shaping 'national security'.
- From proselytising atheists such as Christopher Hitchens, Richard Dawkins and the British Humanist Society, who present sundry arguments against what they perceive as privileged treatment given to formal religion in Britain.
- From the negative perception of churches squabbling amongst themselves over issues such as authority and the acceptance of women in leadership, as well as being entrapped in a prurient preoccupation with sexuality. This combines with the false perception that churches are so empty and irrelevant that they are closing and decaying at great pace.

These challenges to the standing of the institutional churches are multi-directional, and the temptation is to fight back with arguments that can overcome each challenge as it is made. In keeping with the urge to fight back, the advice of the great Japanese ninja master, Yagyu Renya becomes relevant. He pronounces that, 'When an attack does arise, move to meet it swiftly, boldly, and fearlessly. Or better still, make your opponent feel welcome to attack, then capture his spirit when he enters your sphere.'[1] Such an approach is alluring. It would be very satisfying to demonstrate the wrongness of such challenges to the Christian faith, and the imagination and intellect can muster various ways in which this could be achieved. However, whilst there may be many refutations to be had, there is a hazard in adopting a position of opposition. Without thought, the habit of 'tit-for-tat' prevails, and a process is triggered that results in one group being right and the other wrong, and one group being 'in' and the other remaining outsiders, so potentially death-dealing neo-tribalism is furthered.

---

1   See See <http://www.judoinfo.com/quotes3.htm>.

MAKING THINGS WORSE

The risk of exacerbating unhelpful and unholy dynamics is a real one when times are troubled. For this reason alone, reflective practice is important. Reflective practice ensures careful evaluation of the very words and concepts we use to grapple with these challenges. Categories such as opponent, capture, attack, opposition, all come under scrutiny when we are committed to reflective practice. These are values which dominate the Old Testament, but are superseded by Jesus' teaching and practice in the Gospels. However, the Gospels show explicitly how Jesus himself had to struggle to see through the boundary-ridden assumptions which would have encouraged the separation of people into them and us. So when Jesus was confronted by the Canaanite woman – the non-Jew who beseeched Jesus to heal her daughter, Jesus responded in the way his Jewish upbringing had taught him. He was locked in the assumption that the grace of God which he brought was for the Jews alone. It was the woman's refusal to trade insults with him, her capacity to resist tit for tat, which enabled Jesus to break out of the way in which he had been taught to construe the world. The category of the Jews as 'Chosen People' fell away, and for the first time Jesus articulates a new inclusive concept: that we are all God's children. This story in Matthew 15:21–28, powerfully illustrates the significance of the categories we use to make sense of our world and our place within it. It also highlights how followers of Jesus need to be open to the learning that comes from encounters with those who are different from us, and who invite us to see beyond our efforts to maintain boundaries and perpetuate clannishness.

In addition to learning from the practices which Jesus demonstrated, reflective practice also encourages learning from the accumulated wisdom of our Christian forbears. Saints and religious sages throughout the centuries have lived lives that have been characterised by the sometimes costly letting go of ego and self-interest, which exemplified alternative processes to those of tit for tat. However, in our hyper-anxious, troubled times, even this store of wisdom has to be used cautiously. For centuries the commitment and example of Christian martyrs has been lauded, but today the word 'martyr' prompts hideous anxiety in people. In a dystopian world the concept of martyr is associated with furious religion, which seeks to deliver 'God's revenge' on those who are different in faith and practice. The notion of martyrdom as the ultimate expression of passive resistance has been lost, as those who embrace martyrdom for the sake of their faith are now seen as a threat to peaceable living, rather than as founts of wisdom.

PATIENTLY ATTENDING

In troubled times it is unhelpful to 'oppose' because it feeds fragmentation and neo-tribalism, but, if we are not to fight and resist, what else is to be done? Clearly, if there is urgency to become effective in encouraging people to learn from the way Jesus lived, as a way of surmounting troubled times, Christians cannot just sit back. Reflective practice can offer a way forward by providing alternative approaches to the three challenges to Christian faith that were identified earlier. Reflective practice requires openness to the possibility that some truth is to be gleaned from the challenges made to the way the Christian faith has been expressed, both in the past and in the present day. A commitment to reflective practice means being open to the possibility that those who oppose may bring a gift of insight, but this requires a willingness to listen well and listen long, even though such *patient attentiveness*[2] may be a painful experience.

Ernst Bloch, in his magnum opus *The Principle of Hope*,[3] urges us to seek out the emancipatory and utopian potential that he suggests is present within all manifestations of everyday and cultural life. He suggests that a 'utopian surplus' is always present in human enterprise, because human yearning to transform the world, or to be set free from all that diminishes, is so deeply rooted that it is discernible in every expression of culture. This confidence that Bloch has in the deep-seated, unquenchable urge towards hope is similar to what process theology refers to as *God's lure*. In process theology God is not a God of intervention, but rather a God who lures us towards his will. In response to God's lure, and in following Bloch's urge to seek out the hope-giving element to be

2   Patient attentiveness was a term used by Archbishop Rowan Williams in his presidential address to the General Synod of the Church of England, July 2005.
3   E. Bloch, *The Principle of Hope*, Cambridge, MA: MIT Press, 1986.

found in cultural expression, there needs to be a willingness to listen well and listen long.

Listening well and listening long are aspects of the hospitality which runs as a theme throughout the New Testament, and to an extent through the books of the Old Testament. Hospitality involves more than treating the stranger generously, it is also about hearing and listening generously and openly. For example, hospitality to the thoughts of Samuel Huntington, by listening well and listening long, brings insights that are important to the task of enacting hope. Samuel Huntington's analysis is straightforward and compelling, and it has the world faiths, particularly Christianity and Islam, in its sights. Because Huntington's analysis is so appealing and straightforward, it is regularly harnessed by media commentators to support the case that religion is disruptive to peaceable relations.

Significantly, Huntington spelt out this analysis in the early 1990s, a decade before the events of 11 September 2001. The actions of the religiously motivated terrorists were explained as an expression of fury at the values and practices associated with advanced Western, and especially American, 'civilisation'. After the dust had settled, Huntington had become a prophet for our time, and people who took their faith seriously, and sought to advance their faith, had, for many, become the pariahs of our time. However, by listening well and listening long, as reflective practice encourages, it becomes clear that Huntington nuanced his analysis. He noted that other factors have contributed to the Islamic resurgence and the Western–Islamic clash, in particular the factor of the demographic profile of many Islamic countries and communities. Huntington also cites the values of Western universalism, i.e. the view that all civilisations should adopt Western values, and it is this that infuriates youthful Islamic fundamentalists. He writes:

> I don't think Islam is any more violent than any other religions, and I suspect if you added it all up, more people have been slaughtered by Christians over the centuries than by Muslims. But the key factor is the demographic factor. Generally speaking, the people who go out and kill other people are males between the ages of 16 and 30.[4]

---

4   M. Steinberger, 'So, are Civilizations at War?', interview with Samuel P. Huntington, *The Observer*, 21 October 2001.

History supports Huntington's recognition of the capacity of young men (and Christians) to kill others, and how a preponderance of young men identifying themselves strongly with a neighbourhood, or nation, or religion, feeds tribalism and can prompt violence against a perceived opposition. Rulers throughout history have regularly harnessed the aptitude of young men to go to war and take lives and lose their lives. This later analysis by Huntington, which takes into account the enduring propensity of young men, and not just Muslim or religious young men, toward violence, has been ignored by the media. Nor has the invasive or contagious nature of Western values been scrutinised rigorously. This is not to try and pass the buck, but to emphasise that by listening well and listening long, alternative perspectives emerge that feed the imagination and challenge the dominant perspectives that are perpetuated by clichés that curtail honest thinking. The idea that religion and religious people are dangerous can be accommodated far more comfortably by the media with their secular agenda than a more informed analysis that takes seriously everyone's capacity to foster a murderous heart within themselves, particularly at certain stages in our lifespan.

Whilst little is to be achieved by bemoaning this unfairness, there may be some positives to be gained from adopting strategies that take seriously this more nuanced analysis by Huntington. By listening well and listening long the imagination can be engaged, and hope enacted, in relation to vulnerable sixteen- to thirty-year-olds for whom violence comes so naturally. David Lammy MP, as Junior Schools Minister, recounted a conversation 'Why, one boy asked me, was I worried about his grades at school when he might not live long enough to get a job?' Uanu Seshmi, the co-founder of the From Boyhood to Manhood Foundation, when commenting on gang culture, suggests that the willingness to expend life, including one's own, is widely prevalent: 'There is a nihilistic attitude at the moment of helplessness, hopelessness, and, worst of all, of lovelessness.'[5] He went on to comment that from his experience he could also see how, with the right intervention and

---

5   David Lammy's quote and Uanu Seshmi's quotations are both taken from *Children and Young People Now*, 27 August–2 September 2008, 'Quotes of the Week', p. 16.

support, young men can take control of their lives rather than be trapped within a careless neo-tribalism.

Huntington, in his later analysis, provides the foundation for a theory of action that can inform work with young people. Adherents of the Christian and Islamic faiths, by listening well and listening long to Huntington, gain a rigorous rationale for their work with young people. Work with young people becomes a priority for those who take their faith seriously *because* of the propensity of young people, especially young men, to embrace fundamentalist 'right answers' and an associated tribalism. Therefore, extra effort needs to be devoted to providing antidotes to this predilection for right answers, and despising those who see things differently. Gwen Griffith-Dickson, founder of the Lokahi Foundation,[6] notes that to counter the potential for murderous intent associated with intense religious fundamentalism, skill is needed at bringing emotional arousal down *and* fostering critical, reflective capacities. She identifies how high levels of emotion tend to knock out a person's, especially a young person's, critical faculties.[7] With high levels of emotional arousal it becomes difficult for people to 'process', i.e. to hear without reacting, information that counters their perception. This gives further endorsement to the importance of reflective practice when seeking to enact hope in worrisome times.

More recent critics of religion, such as Dawkins and Hitchins, are harder to listen to well and long, because there is a bitterness that accompanies their critique, which has an explicit aim to bring religion down. Nevertheless, they carry a clear message from which Christians can learn. It is the message that faith can go wrong. Christians have to own up to the fact that there is a danger associated with strong and passionate faith, and acknowledge that people of faith can be death-dealing as well as life-giving. Theologians have given little attention to the vital distinction between healthy and unhealthy religion.[8] Believers as well as

---

6   Lokahi (loh-kah-hee) is a Hawaiian word. It means harmony, unity and balance which arises from diversity and even opposition. See <http://www.lokahi.org.uk/>.

7   Professor G. Griffith-Dickson, Lecture to the Faith & Public Policy Forum at King's College London, 2 October 2007.

8   William James was one of the first people to distinguish between healthy and unhealthy religion in his book *The Varieties of Religious Experience* first published in 1902.

unbelievers have always known that things can go wrong with religion, but believers have been reluctant to own up to it. The fact that it has taken critics such as Huntington, Dawkins and Hitchins to flush out this reality is quite shameful.

'What people believe can uplift their lives and make them strong, or it can steal life, clouding it with guilt and all kinds of distortions. It can divide communities, one from another and religion, too often in history, has been the rationale for war.' This was the opening sentence of a sermon preached by Ron Sebring.[9] In this sermon he went on to analyse what happened in Jonestown in Guyana, under the leadership of Jim Jones, when 914 people committed mass suicide. Sebring notes that Jim Jones was well educated and belonged to a mainstream denomination, so these factors were not protectors against unhealthy religion. Sebring draws significance from Jones preaching about things to hate and things to be against. He comments that unhealthy religion tends to draw its strength from having an enemy, and as a result of having identified an 'evil' out there, people can be coaxed and encouraged to make 'a stand'. Sebring concludes that religion obsessed with an 'evil' is suspect, including even the milder forms of negativity associated with finger pointing, backbiting and self-righteous indignation.

HEALTHY RELIGION

Sebring lists some of the characteristics of healthy religion, and the first item on his list relates to critical reflectiveness:

- Healthy religion does not indoctrinate, but teaches people to think for themselves.
- Healthy religion invites us to be humble about what we believe and what we know.
- Healthy religion does not invest in negativity; it does not major on what it is against but rather on what it is for.
- Healthy beliefs stay in tune with reality, never filling in gaps for what we do not know.

---

9   Sermon Preached at Northbrae Community Church, Berkeley, California, 22 May 2005, by Ron Sebring.

Sebring's commentary on what happened in Jonestown in 1977 invites reflection on *how* people embrace faith. So far such reflection has not percolated the evangelistic efforts associated with Decades of Evangelism or 'Fresh Expressions' or 'Mission Shaped Church', nor has the exploration of what makes for healthy or unhealthy faith been given space in the training of faith leaders. The Commission on Urban Faith and Life, which revisited similar terrain to the report *Faithful Cities*, began to map out what would be the markers of unhealthy and healthy religion. The Commission focused on this because 'religion' can fracture the social cohesion that is essential to the life of globalising cities. In the Commission's report *Faithful Cities* four hallmarks of healthy religion were identified:

• It will enlarge the imagination.
• It will teach and encourage the practice of wisdom and holiness.
• It will open us to the new.
• It will deepen our sympathies.[10]

These four hallmarks, along with those identified by Sebring, provide way markers for the challenge Christians and churches face in coping with the 'dip' in the J-Curve. Reflective practice is essential if the hallmarks of healthy religion are to be achieved. Reflective practice requires sympathy for the other, a willingness to embrace what is new or emerging, and the self-discipline and self-understanding that come from the practice of wisdom and holiness.

EMBRACING SYSTEMIC THINKING

Underneath these four features or hallmarks of healthy religion is not just a commitment to reflective practice but also skill in relation to 'systemic' thinking. Systemic or systems thinking is both simple and complex. At one extreme, systemic thinking is the energiser of the discipline of cybernetics with all its complexity, but systems thinking is also intuitive: 'For want of a nail, the shoe was lost; for

---

10   *Faithful Cities*, the Report of the Commission on Urban Life and Faith, London: Church House Publishing and Methodist Publishing House, 2006, p. 84. These four hallmarks were first articulated by a group facilitated by Bishop John Austin in Birmingham.

want of the shoe, the horse was lost; for want of the horse, the rider was lost; for want of the rider, the message was lost; for want of the message, the victory was lost; for want of the victory, the kingdom was lost; and all for the want of a nail' (trad.). Systems thinking is also at the heart of Christian thinking. When St Paul is confronted by the quarrels and disputes at Corinth he offers the image of a body with many parts as a means of encouraging unity despite difference: 'As it is, there are many parts, but one body.'[11] Paul, having commended this systems approach in which the parts and whole are intricately interrelated, then goes on to write one of most inspiring passages in any of his many letters: 'And now I will show you the most excellent way[12] … And now these three remain, faith, hope and love. But the greatest of these is love.'[13] Love is the means by which all that is different is held together, because love, more than hope and faith, has an outward dynamic.

A systemic approach to seeing and understanding the world is a practical expression of love, because a systems perspective refuses to isolate one thing, or group or individual, but appreciates the inter-connectedness of life, acknowledging that everything interacts with and impacts on the things around it. A systems approach recognises the interwoven nature of all aspects of life, so the grief or pain felt in one part, or by one party, is both perceptibly and imperceptibly felt by all. The essential story of our world is that of connectedness and systems thinking maintains this recognition and endeavours to respect the intricate interrelationship and mysterious connections between events, people and the creation itself. Systems thinking acknowledges our interdependence. Things, events, people cannot be understood in isolation, because things, or parts, function the way they do because of other 'parts'. It is not too great a leap of the imagination to suggest that the dynamic that holds things together in such intricate interrelationship is love.

In dismal times, systems thinking is vital. The great virtue of systems thinking is that it safeguards against two troublesome dynamics that gain momentum when people are anxious – the urge to blame and the urge to separate into 'them and us', which thus give energy to 'distancing' and the neo-tribalism that was referred to

---

11 1 Cor 12:20.
12 1 Cor 12:31.
13 1 Cor 13:13.

earlier. Systems thinking resists blaming because of the recognition that when something goes wrong, the interconnectedness of our world means that the problem belongs with the system and not with an individual or group of individuals. The great 2008 collapse of the banking system prompted a rash of blaming, but even here systems thinking will help resist this temptation. Robert Pojasek, a sustainable development specialist at Harvard recommends that in order to take seriously the interconnectedness of our world, and recognise the inappropriateness of thinking in terms of a *root* cause on which blame can be poured, one has to ask the question 'Why?' five times. And when the question 'why?' has been applied five times, at some point an answer will include my self-interest and your self-interest. 'I have seen the enemy – and it is us.' These are the words put into the mouth of Pogo, the US cartoon character devised by Walt Kelly. After posing the question 'Why?' five times about the massive failure of banks and hedge funds, before long two or three patterns will emerge, and in all likelihood one pattern will be to do with '*us*'. You and I have added to the inclination of banks and the money-making industry to have acted as they have done.

The process of the five 'Whys?' also makes clear how capitalism implicates you and me. Gough, writing on the parallels between capitalism and Christendom, notes how, in our world, capitalism has taken over from Christendom in becoming all-encompassing and demonstrating unchallengeable power. This feeds the inclination to see capitalism as arrogant and thus the focus of much fury. However, Gough comments that rather than arrogance,

> The extraordinary thing about capitalism is its humility and refusal to judge. It will give us what we want; it will not force on us what it thinks we need. Often we are disgusted by what we discover that we want – but that reflects on us, not on the servant who brings us our fetish gear and saturated fats. It would bring us organic turnips just as happily.[14]

Sin is lurking somewhere in here, sin that runs through each of our hearts. Systemic thinking enables a more thorough-going understanding of sin to develop. In particular it fosters recognition of our complicity in sinful systems. Stan Saunders and Charlie Campbell,

---

14　J. Gough 'The Sacred Mystery of Capitalism', *Prospect*, July 2008, p. 40.

both academic theologians, spent three months working with homeless people and found that they began to see and understand sin quite differently as a result:

> I suspect I started to volunteer to serve breakfast to the homeless as a way of being a more faithful disciple. I did not volunteer to have my heart broken. However, at the basement door I have come not to a greater confidence in my own good works, but to a deeper awareness of my personal sins and my complicity in sinful systems, as well as to a greater dependence on the grace of Jesus Christ.[15]

What happened was that each day homeless people had to be turned away because there was no more room, or because they arrived too late for the meal. Saunders and Campbell became more and more aware of how, despite the many joyful and positive encounters with homeless people, their best efforts at provision fell short. It led to a profound insight,

> What a revelation this has been! I had always assumed that discipleship followed the confession of sin and the acceptance of forgiveness. The faltering hospitality offered via the basement door has taught me that the process is actually reversed: we do not fully know the depth of our sin and the reality of God's grace until we follow the way of Jesus.[16]

When we begin to sense the significance of sinful systems, we get off the back of the poor or marginalised because we see their situation in a new light, and likewise we begin to get an insight into our own culpability. Systemic thinking unravels the usual view of where 'the problem' lies. Systemic thinking is alert to the dynamics of power, so as well as the discipline of asking the question 'Why?' five times in relation to a single issue, systemic thinking also encourages a threefold quiz regarding the exercise of power:

- Who decides?

---

15   S. Saunders and C. Campbell, *The Word on the Street*, Grand Rapids, MI: Erdmans, 2000, p. 2
16   Ibid. p. 3.

- Who wins?
- Who loses?

In every situation there is someone, or some group, who is in one of these positions. In all situations there will be a person or group for whom responsibility for deciding can be allocated. Likewise there will always be some who do better out of a situation than others. Fine. This kind of dynamic is inevitable and unproblematic. However, systemic thinking encourages alertness to patterns and may discover a pattern that shows the same people are repeatedly deciding, gaining or losing. It is at this point that systemic thinking embraces the critical thinking that is often cloaked in the grandiose expression 'the hermeneutic of suspicion', or more colloquially, to smell a rat. Because at this point a 'structure', or an embedded pattern of relationships, may be detected. However, the repeated exercise of power has the capacity to disappear behind a smokescreen. The ability to exercise power regularly over others brings with it the mysterious capacity to disable the onlooker's imagination. It is this capacity which has led some to challenge the inclination of many people of goodwill repeatedly to pose the question 'Why are the poor poor?' The suggestion is that a more astute, systemic analysis would also pose the question how do the rich or the advantaged *maintain* their capacity to be rich or advantaged?[17] Or, to put this more technically, how is structural advantage (an embedded pattern of relationships) maintained?

This highlights the capacity of systemic thinking to turn the telescope around, and Christians as much as others need this skill. The habit of focusing on the needs of the poor is to see only half of the problem, and as a result removes the issues of the increasing affluence of the non-poor and the growth of the hyper-rich out of the frame. Those involved in the networks of resistance to global capitalism have, as a result, little time for Christian compassion and

---

17 This encouragement to pose the question how do the advantaged retain their advantage is associated with the analysis maintained by 'social movements' (this is the collective name given to those many and diverse groups, some of which are formal, others informal, that become most visible when they gather around meetings of the G8 or G20). Social movements usually unite around opposition to capitalism because of the repeated patterns of deciding, wining and losing.

our preoccupation with the needy, because we are viewed as having been bamboozled and co-opted by the powerful, to distract attention from the ways in which 'structural advantage' is maintained. Interestingly, this challenge from the anarchists, bohemians and anti-globalisationists, and others who make up the list of social movements, carries, as Ernst Bloch suggests, an emancipatory aspect for Christians. For it reminds us of the Old Testament prophets of the eighth century BCE such as Amos, Hosea and Micah, who also protested that the rich are the cause of poverty and that the growing distress of the poor indicates how the rich have turned their backs on God.

By taking on board a wider horizon of interrelationships, systemic thinking shows up the way the sinews of power do their work. The powerful are able to maintain their power as a result of:

- the ability to define and give legitimacy to roles and rules;
- the provision of rewards for performing well in these roles;
- the practice of including or co-opting those who operate the rules effectively;
- the use of institutional violence against those who fail to deliver, or question or disrupt the status quo. Institutional violence can range from sullying a person's reputation, to exclusion and crucifixion.

There is more than a hint of despair in relation to this model of power and its application, in part because the people in a position to include and reward often feel powerless themselves. But the process of systemic thinking has to be persisted with beyond this analysis, otherwise the trap of 'them and us' thinking opens up, enticing people to blame those perceived to benefit most from the interconnected pattern of structural advantage. If systemic thinking is forsaken too early, then the assumption that gains momentum is that all that is necessary is to overthrow the powerful in order to redeem the future. Throughout history there have been ideological and religious movements that have naively assumed that they are the ultra-virtuous group that can put an end to the repeating pattern of advantage and disadvantage. It is very tempting, particularly in dystopian times, to fall for an analysis that assumes virtue in some and malevolence and mischief in others. This is the route to scapegoating, which, like all bloodletting, may at first appear to bring relief.

JESUS SAVES?

How does God 'plan' to save the world? As I wrote that sentence
I became aware of its foolishness. So many elements of that sentence
are unknowable and unable to be expressed by our own or any
language. Nevertheless we believe we have pointers and John
3:16–17 is one of them. 'For God so loved the world that he gave
his one and only Son, that whoever believes in him shall not perish
but have eternal life. For God did not send his Son into the world
to condemn the world, but to save the world through him.' The
distillation of these powerful verses is that to gain eternal life one
needs to believe in Jesus, or, to put it another way, by saying 'yes'
to the belief that salvation comes through Jesus we receive the gift
of everlasting life. No matter how many times we reassemble this
precious offer of salvation, it ends up as one of those unconvincing
self-referential clichés that are convincing to fewer and fewer people.
I am aware that in 'messing' with these hallowed verses from John's
Gospel I enter treacherous terrain. Lives have been lost through the
centuries defending or promoting different interpretations of these
verses. I risk only my reputation (low-level institutional violence) in
suggesting that this formulation at the heart of the Christian faith
has become a major stumbling block in dystopian times.

The idea that just by believing Jesus is the Son of God, sent to save
the world, this opens the door to eternal life, is in postmodern
times easily dismissed as fairy-tale nonsense because of the absence
of anything that anchors it in earthy day-to-day life. This growing
resistance to the authority of a sacred text cannot just be willed
away. This loss of authority must represent the lowest dip in the J-
Curve for Christians and churches, as the touchstone for God's
ultimate action in the world is dismissed as implausible and unconvincing. It is deeply distressing to have to face up to the reality that
the formulas for our faith have become threadbare, and that
precious summaries of the faith have become mantras for a fragment
of the population. However, the good news is that this lack of
respect for the conceptual aspects of the faith can be countered by
the demonstration of the truth of Jesus in the way he lived his life.

David Bosch in *Transforming Mission*[18] alerts Christians in the
West to our longstanding habit of focusing on the salvation that

---

18   D. Bosch, *Transforming Mission*, New York: Orbis, 1991.

comes through the death and resurrection of Jesus. We have allowed the emphasis on 'salvation' to become so dominant in our theology that we are inclined to think that Jesus came on earth to die for our sins, and that this is the great story of the Gospels. However, it is only one aspect of the great story of the Gospels. To move through the dip of the J-Curve towards enacted hope, and go beyond the unconvincing assertion of hope, we embrace the gift of Jesus, who came to show us how to live. Through both his life and through his death Jesus brings salvation. However, if we want to be effective in carrying a message of profound and enduring hope to the world, i.e. to move out of the dip, it is necessary to lessen the emphasis on Jesus bearing our sins on the cross. This shocking suggestion is made because of the inability of most people to make sense of the formula of sins being taken away by a man dying on the cross, having neither a sense of sin nor the ability to grasp the concept of atonement (in its many formulations). When most people *just don't get it*, but a few do, then the slippery slope towards 'I'm alright Jack' gnosticism is a real danger.

What is being said here is that the capacity of Jesus to show us how to live is a God-sent resource for times when people are bothered and bewildered. What is not being said is that the taking away of sin is not true or relevant. It is both true and relevant but it is also implausible and inaccessible. The risk is that if we persist in leading with this aspect of salvation that Jesus brings, we will close off the possibility of people responding to the true and relevant feature of our faith, that Jesus came into the world to show us how to live.

In order to highlight the extraordinary radicalness of Jesus in the way he lived, it is helpful to return to the model of structural advantage which shows the way in which the sinews of power operate. It was noted that there was a hint of despair in relation to this analysis, because, if there is to be any hope, it is reliant on the unlikely ascendancy of a group that can forgo self-interest and sustain virtuous behaviour. Jesus, in the way he lived, subverts this process by which the advantage of some is continually advanced. Jesus shows how it is possible break down our entrapment in the world's systems and step outside the established patterns of power.[19]

---

19   I am indebted to Chris Erskine for these insights.

Jesus' capacity to understand the tricky nature of power perhaps relates to the forty days of testing time in the desert that he endured before embarking on his public ministry. Satan's temptations all invite Jesus to resort to power stratagems, but on each occasion Jesus resists. In the light of his capacity to eschew earthly power, Peter, Jesus' unlikely lieutenant, skates on thin ice when he tries to strengthen Jesus' courage for the fight. In Matthew 16:21, Jesus predicts his own death: 'Jesus began to explain to his disciples how he must go to Jerusalem and suffer many things at the hands of the elders, chief priests and teachers of the law, and that he must be killed ...' We read that Peter took Jesus aside and told him off, perhaps even physically shaking Jesus. Peter, one senses, thought that Jesus was beset by a crisis of morale, and Peter insisted that their challenge to the system would not result in Jesus' death, stating that 'This shall never happen to you.' Jesus turns and says to Peter, 'Out of my sight, Satan! You are a stumbling block to me, you do not have in mind the things of God, but the things of men.'[20]

One cannot but help think that for Jesus, the value Peter gives to worldly or human force reprised his forty-day desert tutorial on the nature of power. Jesus, in rebuking Peter, also makes clear that there is another way of going forward, another way of performing. Jesus then goes on to describe *kenosis,* 'If anyone would come after me, he must deny himself and take up his cross and follow me. For whoever wants to save his life (or soul) will lose it, but whoever loses his life for me will find it. What good will it be for a man if he gains the whole world but forfeits his soul?'[21]

This potency of Jesus and the way he lived his life, and the way in which he understood the dynamics of power, provide the clue as to why there has been such strong inclination in the West to avert our eyes from the radical coherence of the practices that Jesus demonstrated (David Bosch's point). In a Christendom culture, where the church has often lined up with the powerful, to look too closely at Jesus the man would have been far too disruptive. Rather than see the whole story of Jesus' life and teaching, the habit is to cut the story into little pieces and link it according to the themes of the lectionary and the Church Year, so that some things about

---

20 Matthew 16:22–23 (NIV).
21 Matthew 16:24–26 (NIV).

Jesus are regularly repeated and other aspects scarcely acknowledged. The desire for power and status contaminates theology
and the church's teaching and practices as much as it corrupts other
things. As a result, we have majored on the salvation that comes
from Jesus' death and resurrection at the expense of reflecting on
and practising the distinctive ways in which Jesus lived his life.

It is, of course, impossible to disconnect Jesus' life from his
death and resurrection, not least because Jesus frequently spoke
about its significance. The work of René Girard can go some way
to enabling people to give value to the death and resurrection of
Jesus at the same time as pondering the more accessible insights that
are available from the way in which Jesus lived. Girard's reference
point is not self-referential. Rather than referring continually to
evidence and justification from the Bible, Girard wrote from the
perspective of anthropology as well as from modern literature.
Girard's attention to the death and resurrection of Jesus was due
to his interest in the dynamics that lead to scapegoating.[22] In
dystopian times we too have to attend closely to the dynamics of
scapegoating, because of the inclination to look for someone or
some group to blame for our misery.

Girard begins his explanation of the dynamic of scapegoating by
postulating the 'mimetic of desire', which is basically a kind of
jealousy, but with a twist: we learn what is desirable by observing
what others find desirable (mimicry, hence Girard's use of the
word 'mimetic').[23] Having 'caught' our desires from others, we then
fight to obtain it in the economy of scarcity and this means that
everyone wants what only some can have. This in turn produces
a generalised antagonism which focuses on the individual or group
of individuals who seem to be responsible for this societal unease
associated with hopes raised only to be followed by disappointment. The copying behaviour persists and encourages herding
(ganging together) amongst the disappointed and the desire to
destroy those to whom blame is assigned. The vicious riddance of

---

22 See R. Girard, *Violence and the Sacred*, trans. P. Gregory, Baltimore: Johns
    Hopkins University Press, 1977 and R. Girard, *The Scapegoat*, Baltimore:
    Johns Hopkins University Press, 1986.

23 The 'mimetic of desire' or copying, tallies with Richard Layard's expla-
    nation as to why wealth does not sustain well-being which will be
    discussed in chapter 5.

the victim has the potential to reduce the eagerness for violence, and if not, then the assumption is that more scapegoats need to be sacrificed in order to achieve a sense of appeasement and restoration of the status quo. The removal of the victim or victims – the lambs to the slaughter – gives a temporary re-assurance of the crisis disappearing, and the sensation of renewed possibility. This is indeed cheap hope.

Girard makes an anthropological rather than an ethical point when he focuses on the efficacy of scapegoating, and the shoddy solidarity that is achieved by lynching and banishment. Scapegoating seems to make us feel better – but at immense cost. All of us look for someone to blame, blaming appears as natural as the air we breathe. We know that when people are bothered and bewildered a contagious urge takes hold, so the urge to expose and set upon the vulnerable and those who are different results in a longed for social cohesion. Tragically, there is plenty of evidence in our recent history to support Girard's analysis of death-dealing as a means to uniting around a single goal: the treatment of Jews, gypsies and homosexuals in Nazi Germany, the Rwandan genocide in 1994 and the degrading of indigenous people, are scarcely sufficient examples. The challenge that faces pastoral care in dismal times is to help us become robust enough in relation to systemic thinking to be able to resist this age-old temptation to seek out someone to blame and the ensuing socially cathartic bloodlust.

Girard concludes his anthropological and literary analysis by examining Judeo-Christian texts, and traces the movement away from the dynamic of scapegoating through the Old into the New Testaments. It was this experience that contributed to Girard's conversion to the Christian faith. His analysis of the Bible 'as literature' led him to conclude that:

- Jesus is the *final* scapegoat'.
- The New Testament is 'on the side of' Jesus, the scapegoat. The Gospels are unusual because here is literature that encourages people to see the world through the eyes of the scapegoat.
- The scapegoat in the Gospels refuses to let death be the final word and he rises again triumphant.
- The followers of the scapegoat enact the seizing of the scapegoat, and the scapegoat's triumph over death, in Eucharistic celebration.

This causes Girard to rejoice, because this is the literature, with an associated enacted process (the Eucharist), which exposes a fundamental dimension of violence.[24] When we understand how a myth such as blaming and scapegoating works, it loses its power over us. This insight helps foster reflective rather than reactive behaviour, and holds off the urge for neo-tribalism and its high potential for resentment, hatred and bloodlust.

It is at this point we have the coming together of mission and pastoral care. An important aspect of the salvation that Jesus brings to us is insight into our hatred and murderous behaviour, and this is a timely gift in our dystopian context. The missionary challenge is to find creative ways of helping people to explore this insight, and the pastoral challenge is to help people appropriate, or take this gift of insight into their (our) practice. Access to these insights is not via belief but rather a commitment to reflect on the sacred or special narrative that tells of Jesus. This shift from investment in 'belief' to acknowledging the everyday relevance of the story of Jesus, both through his life, death and resurrection, is the point at which mission and pastoral care coalesce.

Down in the dip, when things seem to be going from bad to worse, the recommended practice that Jesus commends and demonstrates is to *give* one's self away. Jesus' death on the cross expresses his ultimate self-giving. However, this was only one aspect of *kenosis*, Jesus also lived *practising and demonstrating kenosis*. By heeding both these aspects of kenosis we can both subvert the quiet tyranny that keeps structural advantage in place, and ease the inclination to blame and scapegoat those whom we perceive to be standing in the way of our desires. The mission, and specifically evangelistic challenge, is to help people to reflect on the plausibility

---

24 Walter Wink in his *Powers* trilogy likewise rejoices in the capacity of the Gospels, and particularly the actions and teaching of Jesus to unmask scapegoating, oppression and death-dealing. See W. Wink's *Powers* trilogy: 'Naming the *Powers: The Language of Power in the New Testament*, Philadelphia: Fortress Press, 1984; *Unmasking the Powers: The Invisible Forces that Determine Human Existence*, Philadelphia: Fortress Press, 1986; and *Engaging the Powers: Discernment and Resistance in a World of Domination*, Minneapolis: Fortress Press, 1992. In *The Powers that Be: Theology for a New Millennium* (1999), New York: Doubleday, Wink unites his thinking in a single volume.

of following Jesus in the practice of kenosis, and the challenge in relation to pastoral care is to help people experiment with the practical viability of the self-giving that is at the heart of kenosis.

4 Investing in an Alternative Economy

For Homo sapiens, the idea of scarcity is deeply embedded. Our evolutionary journey has been characterised as a battle against shortage, resulting in a deep-seated assumption that the good things in life are in short supply. It is a short step to assume that the purpose of our lives is to rise to the challenge of gathering these things for ourselves and our household or tribe, before others can get hold of them. This pushiness and associated defendedness is assumed to be a sensible and even laudable strategy for achieving and maintaining security in life. If our view of the world is that it is a place of scarcity and peril, some skills and aptitudes become greatly prized:

- a clever strategic mind, able to work at a level of thinking that is abstracted from reality (it might be called planning!);
- an eye for assessing friend and foe, strength and weakness, ability and inability;
- resisting challenges to our own point of view and self-interest;
- A habit of assuming that one exists in a context of mistrust and threat;
- investment in looking after 'me and mine'.[1]

In dystopian times we are driven not just further into 'scarcity thinking', but risk becoming entrapped in 'survival thinking', where the dominant perspective is that life is dangerous, with hyper alertness to danger and risk. The inclination, therefore, is to exercise defensive tactics with even more intensity and to resort to the anxiety-ridden tactic of accumulating resources. This is the last thing that the world

---

1   These items are informed by R.S. Zander and B. Zander, *The Art of Possibility*, London: Penguin, 2000, especially the chapter 'Stepping into a Universe of Possibility', pp. 17–23

needs, and it is anathema to salvation in the fullest sense of healing the world. It is also the very opposite of the self-emptying way in which Jesus showed us and urged us how to live.

The case that is being made here is that Jesus repeatedly invites us to engage with a different economy from that of the economy of scarcity. However, our habits and paucity of imagination incline us to think that Jesus, in his insistence that there is an economy (i.e. a coherent system) that is not about shortage, was being heavenly minded rather than earthly minded. Jesus' promise of life in all its fullness, where we do not live by bread alone, suggests that the world, here and now, is a place of generous possibility. However, such a promise becomes laughable in a worried, troubled world that has fixated on material resources.

At this point it is necessary to introduce the idea of a 'threshold concept'. Threshold concepts are coming under the spotlight in relation to the teaching of undergraduates. Undergraduates are in a halfway house, or liminal state, in that they need both close teaching and tutoring to impart the content of their area of study, but the hope is that they will also begin to think for themselves in relation to the subject they are studying. The aim is that they become reflective and creative in their thinking, rather than persist in learning by rote. The idea of threshold concepts is introduced here because it provides a clue about how to make sense of and partake of the generous economy to which Jesus invites us.

A threshold concept has the following characteristics:

- A threshold concept is likely to be irreversible. Once it has been grasped it doesn't unravel or get forgotten. It may be built upon, or even modified, but it remains a key element in one's understanding.
- A threshold concept enables other ideas to be linked up, enabling the interconnected nature of phenomena to be sensed.
- A threshold concept opens up a new vista that becomes part of who we are, influencing how we see and how we react and feel. In other words, it becomes part of our biography. In the jargon, a threshold concept brings an ontological shift. It is a bit like an initiation from which one can only move forward.
- A threshold concept can sometimes 'congeal' and become formulaic.
- A threshold concept is unlikely to be complicated, but it may well be 'counter-intuitive' and, for this reason, it can be 'troublesome

knowledge' because it requires common sense thinking to be reversed and this is sometimes deeply uncomfortable and unstable, in the sense that the new concept can come and go until it is confidently applied.[2]

Jesus, in urging us to embrace the self-emptying practice of kenosis, is dealing with a threshold concept. It is 'troublesome knowledge' because it conflicts with common sense, and it remains troublesome even when fully understood and embraced, because it requires sustained confidence in the power of generosity. To illustrate this I offer one of those cheery allegorical stories that circulate between email contacts, often accompanied by the instruction 'to pass it on to those whom you care about'.

A holy man was having a conversation with God one day and said, 'God, I would like to know what Heaven and Hell are like.' God led the holy man to two doors. He opened one of the doors and the holy man looked in.

In the middle of the room was a large round table. In the middle of the table was a large pot of stew, which smelled delicious and made the holy man's mouth water. The people sitting around the table were thin and sickly. They appeared to be famished. They were holding spoons with very long handles, that were strapped to their arms and each found it possible to reach into the pot of stew and take a spoonful. But because the handle was longer than their arms, they could not get the spoons back into their mouths. The holy man shuddered at the sight of their misery and suffering.

God said, 'You have seen Hell.'

They went to the next room and opened the door. It was exactly the same as the first one. There was the large round table with the large pot of stew which made the holy man's mouth water. The people were equipped with the same long-handled spoons, but here the people were well nourished and plump, laughing and talking. The holy man said, 'I don't understand.'

---

2   I am grateful to Liz Thackray for introducing me to the idea of threshold concepts. This exposition of threshold concepts is based on a paper by G. Cousins, 'An Introduction to Threshold Concepts', *Planet*, no. 17, December 2006.

'It is simple,' said God. 'It requires but one skill. You see they have learned to feed each other, while the greedy think only of themselves.'

This rather well-worn story illustrates three things:

1   It illustrates how generosity is inherent in kenosis if it is to be 'performed'.
2   It illustrates the characteristic 'ahaa' that is associated with threshold concepts where the 'the penny has to drop'.
3   It illustrates the habit of associating this kind of kenotic or generous behaviour with heaven, reinforcing the assumption that such generosity is worth aiming for, but that it is scarcely sustainable in the cut and thrust of everyday living.

Jesus, in inviting us to invest in the self-emptying generosity that is at the heart of kenosis, makes not so much an intellectual challenge, or even a moral challenge. Rather, it is a challenge to the imagination. Jesus calls us into the uncomfortable territory of having to ponder 'How will this be?' Here we have an echo of the Annunciation, where the Angel Gabriel greets Mary and informs her that she is highly favoured and will give birth to a Son whose name will be Jesus, and so the conversation goes on until Mary dares to ponder aloud how this will be, given her virginal state.[3] Mary is traditionally lauded for her obedience to God's will. In complex, troubled times, perhaps she should also be lauded for her courage in pondering 'How will this be?' More than obedience, it is this capacity to reflect and engage the imagination that is part of the precious compendium of skills and aptitude that are vital to navigating our bothered and bewildered state.

'How will this be?', or 'How can this be?' is indicative of hesitation, and in a world of scarcity this is a characteristic of a loser. He who hesitates is lost. However, when bothered and bewildered, it is as well to be hesitant. As fragile earthly creatures, we can only hesitantly embrace the radical confidence that can contemplate action that is counter-intuitive. Pausing allows us the time to

---

3   Luke 1:26–38; one suspects that Mary's life was characterised by repeatedly pondering 'how is this to be?'

override our rapidly responding reptile brain,[4] which fires maximally when faced with the possibility of being overwhelmed or losing out. To pause allows time for the neocortex and our 'sapient' capacity to come into play and for courageous and imaginative thinking to follow. For this reason, when struggling with the counter-intuitive realm that Jesus invites us to explore, it is as well to take time to say a little prayer that earns us the space to contemplate an alternative performance from that of narrow, survival thinking.

Mary C. Grey uses the term 'the graced actions of ordinary people' to suggest that such actions 'embody the hope of the coming Kingdom',[5] and I wish to develop this idea of graced actions further.[6] I suggest that 'graced actions' is a good label for those actions which dare to defy the world of scarcity and threat. Graced actions are very different from the skills and aptitudes that are garnered to help one prosper in a world of rivalry and shortage that were described earlier. 'Graced actions' provide a way into the gracious economy, to which Jesus pointed, and they are a way in which it is possible to enact or perform hope in troubled times. Graced actions are a doorway, or, to use the jargon of our time, provide a *portal* into the generous, generative economy of abundance. Whilst the reality of such an alternative economy might prompt a sense of 'how can this be?', graced actions are not so mysterious; they can be reliably and daily performed, but this

---

4   As well as thinking in terms of a triune God, we need also to think in terms of a triune brain. The Reptilian brain (located around the brain stem) is the oldest layer of our brain and is associated with motor movement, appetite, rage, fight and flight. The next layer is referred to as the Old Mammalian brain and is linked with the higher emotions and memory, and the third layer is called the neocortex. Humans and dolphins have developed large neocortices and this area of the brain is associated with the development of language, organisational capacity and reflective ability. It is tempting to conclude that Jesus' teaching and performance, i.e. the new covenant, as well as the manner of his teaching, urge us to make the most of the capacities associated with the neocortex. The old covenant, of the Old Testament, provides a inglorious, graphic illustration of our tussle to rise above our reptilian inclinations!

5   M.C. Grey, *The Outrageous Pursuit of Hope*, London: Darton, Longman and Todd, 2000, p. 10.

6   The original use of the term 'graced action' is from the writings of Thomas Aquinas, and used by the Catholic Church to refer to the seven sacraments: Baptism, Confirmation, Holy Eucharist, Penance, Matrimony, Extreme Unction and Priesthood (Holy Orders).

does not make them mundane, as our efforts at graced actions are our share in Christ's work.

The notion of 'performing' might be a stumbling block for some. The choice of the verb 'perform' is because a graced action calls for imagination and reflection prior to the action. Such conscious thoughtfulness, and even rehearsing in one's mind, is well expressed in the ideas of performing and performance. So in this context, to *perform* a graced action is used in the same sense as to 'carry out'. And it is Jesus' performance of graced actions that provides a storehouse that can feed our imagination and courage to likewise perform graced actions.

WHAT DO 'GRACED ACTIONS' LOOK LIKE?

It is one thing to perform a graced action when all is well in our world, it is quite another to do so when we are bothered and bewildered, and yet it is in such times of trouble and dismay that the ability to perform a graced action is most precious. A graced action begins with the commitment to openness in order to be reflective and seek out all the possibilities in a situation. Only in this way does the imagination have the chance to flow and percolate into the situation. On this basis, gracious *spontaneous* actions are not included in the term 'graced action' because of the emphasis on conscious effort that underpins the way I am using the term. This is not to undervalue spontaneous acts, but rather to highlight the effort that has to be made to harness generosity, imagination and courage in our commitment to live more like Jesus. What is offered below seeks to increase alertness to the potency of generous, well-tuned actions in bringing transformation in dismal and bewildering circumstances.

One imagines that Jesus was caught up in such a situation when he was confronted by the Pharisees and teachers of the law who wanted him to judge the woman whom they said had committed adultery.[7] Jesus, and everyone around in the temple courts, knew that this was a trap. Interestingly, it was a trap because it must have been public knowledge that Jesus would wish to be compassionate towards women and those judged to have offended the sexual

---

7   John 8:2–11.

mores of the time. So what was Jesus to do? He pauses. Jesus has
consciously to think through how he is to perform in this tricky
situation. He has to take time to harness his imagination. He starts
to write with his finger in the sand as they persist in questioning
him. Jesus does not speak. Apocryphal sources have it that Jesus
is writing in the sand the various sins committed by the woman's
accusers. Jesus takes his time, and then stands up and utters that
famous sentence, 'If anyone of you is without sin, let him be the first
to stone her.' He then stoops down and continues to write with his
finger in the sand. We read that the older accusers leave first.
There is plenty of scope to speculate why this might be, and
eventually none of the accusers were left. Jesus then invited the
woman to embrace a new way of being.

Professionalism often gets a bad name, but good professionalism
involves consciously widening the imagination so that the response
that is made to a person's circumstance draws on an imagination
that has been fed by insights accumulated over time.
Professionalism provides a foundation from which the imagination
can flourish – or be inhibited. Skill and knowledge clearly count for
something, but without the imagination professionalism can be
constraining and limiting. Zander and Zander tell of the school-
teacher who shaved her head in order to 'reframe' the circumstances
of a young girl in her class who had lost her hair because of
chemotherapy. As a result of the teacher's action many other
children in the class also had their heads shaved. The professional
understanding of the teacher about how children can be cruel to
those who are different, and her recognition of the young girl's
vulnerability as she coped with mockery and a life-threatening
illness, combined with imagination and commitment. Zander and
Zander describe the teacher's actions as follows:

> (She) intervened on the divisions occurring in her classroom by
> reframing the meaning of the child's strange appearance,
> releasing the little girl from her identity as a feared alien. The
> teacher distinguished baldness as *possibility* [my italics] – a
> fashion statement, and act of choice, a game to play, an act of
> solidarity and connection. No one was made wrong. There was
> nothing to fix.[8]

---

8   Zander and Zander, p. 164.

This graced action by the teacher called everyone in her class, and maybe even beyond, into a new state of being.

A graced action will often give value and significance to the modest and humble. Jesus makes a point of giving value to the poor widow who gave two very small copper coins to the temple treasury. He gave significance to a gift made by someone living in poverty compared with the gift that is given from a position of wealth.[9]

In Craigmillar in Edinburgh the church opened a café within the church building ... Jessie Douglas, a local person, was employed to run the café. Jessie's son had died in a motorbike accident a year and a half before the café opened and from the café's earliest days people came in with stories from their lives – stories of children living with drug addicted parents, stories of housing difficulties and stories of loss. Stories of loss became increasingly common as the community faced a series of tragic deaths – children who lost parents in car accidents and through suicide and murder. People began to ask if they could sit in the church for a while on their own. Eventually people asked if they could have a memorial to those who had died and a group drawn from the church and the wider community decided to make a tree out of copper piping.

People learned how to weld and cut leaves out of copper sheets. The copper tree is a visual symbol of both loss and hope. Often you will find someone sitting in the church because they want to ... and because they find it helps them to be there. Whilst the copper tree was being made a boy of thirteen died in an accident at home. It was devastating for his parents and five brothers and sisters. Soon after, three children, Louise, Calais and Lewis, came in to the café; their parents had been killed in a road accident. From these and other experiences a second project was born, a child bereavement project: 'Richmond's Hope', which gives children a chance to express in therapeutic play the feelings associated with their loss.[10]

---

9   Luke 21:1–4.
10 This story from Craigmillar, written by the Revd Liz Henderson, Minister at Craigmillar Church, is recorded in *Faithful Cites*, the Report of the

This graced action, enabled by the vulnerability and ordinariness of Jesse, was generative, i.e. enabling a sequence of positives in a harsh environment, including enabling those who had experienced profound loss to embrace a new state of being.

Often a graced action allows the context to have authority, which means that law, bureaucracy and tradition have a partial rather than an absolute status. It was on the Sabbath that Jesus was moved by the sight of an old woman whose spine had collapsed; she was doubled over and couldn't straighten herself. It is one of the few instances where Jesus initiated healing. Jesus called to her, he touched her, although the 'spirit' that had crippled her for eighteen years meant that she was unclean. She immediately straightened up and began to thank God. The synagogue ruler was far from happy at this healing in his synagogue on the Sabbath. The rest of the story is best told in the words of Luke's Gospel:

> The Lord answered him, 'You hypocrites! Doesn't each of you on the Sabbath untie his ox or donkey from the stall and lead it to water? Then should not this woman, a daughter of Abraham, whom Satan has kept bound for eighteen long years, be set free on the Sabbath day from what bound her?' When he said this, all his opponents were humiliated, but the people were delighted with all the wonderful things he was doing.[11]

Most certainly, in this instance, law, bureaucracy and tradition were given partial rather than absolute status by Jesus.

> On the central reservation of Wolverhampton's ring road sits a khaki tent with a pair of torn socks drying on a stick outside. Every morning an old man crawls out holding a broom and begins sweeping the kerb which separates him from the passing juggernauts. ... Josef Stawinoga, 83, a Second World War veteran from Poland, has been living in a tent on the grass island for 40 years. Traumatised by war, he has a phobia of confined spaces. The ring road is the only place he feels secure.

Archbishops' Commission on Urban Life and Faith, London: Methodist Publishing/Church House Publishing, 2006, p. 77.
11   Luke 13:10–17.

He believes the Second World War is still being fought and fears strangers are out to harm him. ... Refusing to answer to the name Josef, Mr Stawinoga has become known as Fred. ... Mr Stawinoga's living arrangements have been sanctioned by the town hall. Last week Wolverhampton City Council called in the Territorial Army to erect a ninth replacement tent over the old man's original construction of plastic sheeting. Officials acknowledge that he will live on the intersection for the rest of his life. A spokeswoman said: 'Although this is not an ideal situation it has been accepted as the best option for him, taking into account his personal history and the fact that he can be visited daily by the council's meals on wheels service.'[12]

Jesus had told his disciples that he was going to be betrayed and put to death, but after three days would rise again. The disciples couldn't fully comprehend this, but they clearly got the idea that there was an issue of succession. As they journeyed to Capernaum, Jesus could see that the disciples where arguing between themselves. When they arrived at the house in which they were staying 'He asked them, "What were you arguing about on the road?" But they kept quiet because on the way they had argued about who was the greatest. Sitting down, Jesus called the Twelve and said, "If anyone wants to be first, he must be the very last, and the servant of all."'[13]

There is a story similar to this in Matthew's Gospel. In this instance it is James's and John's mother who approached Jesus to make a claim for their succession rights. And once again Jesus makes clear that to achieve this, one must have confidence in the effectiveness of the 'self-emptying' process that is at the heart of kenosis. To confirm his wish that the relationship between his disciples should not be like 'The rulers of the Gentiles (who) lord it over them, and their high officials (who) exercise authority over them',[14] Jesus carries out a remarkable symbolic act. Jesus insists on washing their feet, thus providing an imaginative and forever

---

12 A. Chrisafis, 'Territorial Army Provides Home Improvements for Wolverhampton's Ring Road Hermit', *The Guardian*, 16 April 2003. Mr Stawinoga died in October 2007 at the age of eighty-six.
13 Mark 9:30–35 NIV.
14 Matthew 20:25 NIV.

memorable lesson that the relationships between the disciples are to be characterised by lowly attentiveness.

> When he had finished washing their feet, he put on his clothes and returned to his place. 'Do you understand what I have done for you?' he asked them. 'You call me 'Teacher' and 'Lord', and rightly so, for that is what I am. Now that I, your Lord and Teacher have washed your feet, you should wash one another's feet. I have set you an example that you should do as I have done for you'.[15]

Alcoholics Anonymous may well be the largest and most effective process of church in the land. Six of the twelve steps commended to the alcoholic, who wishes to move to the humble status of 'recovering', invite the alcoholic to turn to God. Less well known than the twelve steps are the twelve traditions that outline how Alcoholics Anonymous operates. I present all twelve traditions because their clarity and simplicity are an example of commitment to self-giving, rather than the accumulation of status and power. They are an extraordinary embodiment of graced action within an organisation:

Tradition One
Our common welfare should come first; personal recovery depends on A.A. unity.

Tradition Two
For our group purpose there is but one ultimate authority – a loving God as He may express Himself in our group conscience. Our leaders are but trusted servants; they do not govern.

Tradition Three
The only requirement for A.A. membership is a desire to stop drinking.

Tradition Four
Each group should be autonomous except in matters affecting other groups or A.A. as a whole.

---

15   John 13:12–15 NIV.

Tradition Five
Each group has but one primary purpose – to carry its message to the alcoholic who still suffers.

Tradition Six
An A.A. group ought never to endorse, finance, or lend the A.A. name to any related facility or outside enterprise lest problems of money, property, and prestige divert us from our primary purpose.

Tradition Seven
Every A.A. group ought to be fully self-supporting, declining outside contributions.

Tradition Eight
Alcoholics Anonymous should remain forever non-professional, but our service centres may employ special workers.

Tradition Nine
A.A. as such, ought never to be organised; but we may create service boards or committees directly responsible to those they serve.

Tradition Ten
Alcoholics Anonymous has no opinion on outside issues; hence the A.A. name ought never to be drawn into public controversy.

Tradition Eleven
Our public relations policy is based on attraction rather than promotion; we need always maintain personal anonymity at the level of press, radio, and films.

Tradition Twelve
Anonymity is the spiritual foundation of our traditions, ever reminding us to place principles before personalities.[16]

---

16   These 'Twelve Steps and Twelve Traditions' are taken (with permission) from a book of that name which can be obtained from AA General Service Office, PO Box 1, Stonebow House, Stonebow, York YO1 2NJ, Tel. 01904 644026.

Graced actions trigger a host of other virtuous actions and behaviour in others, in this way graced actions are *generative*, giving momentum to the divine, or abundant economy in which, through God's grace, and through Jesus' tutorship, we are invited to partake. We have to embrace the discipline of reflection, the gift of inspiration or imagination, and an ability to be non-conformist in relation to dominant assumptions of value and priority. The graced actions described above exemplify these elements in order to *earth* the concept of enacted or performed hope. It is important to note that graced actions are not limited to Christians. Generosity of spirit, imagination, courage, stepping outside convention are all capacities displayed by people of other faiths and none. The scope to invest in the alternative economy of abundance is not just for Christians; it is open to all and can be energised by everyone who dares to make a leap of faith beyond the limitations of the economy of scarcity.

Graced actions are relevant to the J-Curve analysis described in chapter 2. Graced actions contribute to the enacting of hope. The generative nature of graced actions means that the commitment to enacting hope carries momentum towards virtuous progression. A hopeful act may be a solitary phenomenon, but it may also trigger a host of other hope-giving acts. In dismal times we anticipate vicious processes dominating our lives, but graced actions defy this negative view of the world. Graced actions insist that hope is not just a reality, but virtuous beyond our anticipation. Hope can indeed cascade and it is this that is represented by the higher right side of the J-Curve. Whilst it is possible to retreat from the dip of the J-Curve by scooting up the left side, which involves investing more and more in self-referential formulaic expression of faith and asserted hope, moving to the expansive right side means investment in reflection, imagination and action informed by the way in which Jesus lived.

TRIPPED UP BY ANXIETY

The greatest obstruction to graced actions is anxiety, and in times when people are bothered and bewildered anxiety mounts. If graced actions that enact hope are to be fostered, then helping people to counter acute and chronic anxiety becomes a pastoral priority. Peter L. Steinke comments that, 'The survival brain's strength is quickness, but its speed is at the expense of the thinking brain's accuracy. During anxious times, instinct overpowers intention and impulse eliminates reflection. People react rather than respond. They "pull the trigger" of the survival reaction quickly and thoughtlessly.'[17] And there we have it, unacknowledged anxiety cuts across the ability to reflect, and reflection is the starting point of graced actions.

Crudely, anxiety comes in two forms: acute anxiety which is situational and triggered by crises or irritations. It is temporary in nature, and given time we rise above the anxious response. Chronic anxiety, on the other hand, is ongoing and habitual. So whilst anxiety is meant to function as an alarm or warning signal, the ever-presence of chronic anxiety means that it becomes a normative state and the person ceases to recognise its impact. Anxiety also affects our perceptions, and it also prompts us to act on these perceptions. So whilst the perceptions might not have been rooted in reality, the response does create a new and more troubled reality. This unholy dynamic begins because unhinged or unacknowledged anxiety looks for scapegoats, i.e. someone or some group to blame for the discomfort that is a product of anxiety (as discussed in chapter 3). Often it is a minority group that gets blamed, or youngsters, where an entire group gets blamed on the basis of misdemeanours by a small proportion. The anxious and aggrieved look for alliances, in order to share and energise the grievance, and before long hatred is generated. In the context of the neo-tribalism that Bauman suggests takes hold in our globalising and fragmented world, this provides fertile ground for destructive dynamics. Unacknowledged anxiety doesn't just lead to graced actions drying up; it also inhibits the ability to see the world, the Creation, as a whole, with an intricate and mysterious interconnectedness. However, anxiety is not the last word.

The good news about anxiety is that there are antidotes to both the chronic and acute forms. There are a number of *spiritual* habits to cultivate, and in which to coach others, in the art of anxiety reduction:[18]

---

17 P.L. Steinke, 'Changing Emotional Systems', *Congregations*, no. 2, Spring 2004.

18 I consider the impact of anxiety on our behaviour and attitudes to be fundamental. This section on anxiety is based on previous expositions on anxiety that I have made, particularly in *Journeying Out*, pp. 184–94.

- *To become aware of one's own reactive buttons.* These are (metaphorical) buttons that people can press inadvertently and they put us on edge. These often have their root in our family or community of origin. Each of us will have our own constellation of reactive buttons that continually trigger unwarranted reactions. But being aware of our own, idiosyncratic buttons earns us a second's grace that allows reaction to become a response, i.e. time becomes available to enable reflection.
- *To discipline both our heads and hearts that problems have multiple and interrelated causes.* To settle on the idea that there is a single cause is to do violence to our intricate and interrelated world. Our existence is shaped by 'systems' in which the emphasis is on interrelatedness, rather than single or isolated events. This 'systems' approach is essential if we are to prevent ourselves from falling prey to scapegoating.
- *A determination to resist picking up other people's anxieties.* This requires a distinction to be made between listening and hearing people's gripes, but not siding with them or getting caught up in the process of herding. The aim, rather, is to encourage people to take responsibility for their own feelings. When your ear is bent by someone who relates a substantial litany of offences that have been committed against them, the response might be: 'What do you think *you* need to do for the best?'
- *Develop the capacity to be a 'non-anxious presence'.* Firstly, this involves logging our own anxiety. Only when we can sense and track our own anxiety do we have any chance of reducing it. Then it is possible to 'park' that anxiety – consciously putting it out of the way. There is a Buddhist practice that can help us locate that 'parking space' for anxiety. It involves *softening* our eyes. When we are anxious our eyes become hard and they also look hard, hence the expressions 'Stop eyeballing me' or 'Get out of my face.' When we soften our eyes we increase the likelihood of responding calmly rather than reacting with our cold-blooded reptile brain. Buddhists recommend that softening the eyes becomes part of the discipline of prayerfulness. It is part of the quietening that helps us to be more open to God and to each other. For those who are bemused by the bidding to soften our eyes, there is a clue to the process. If it is difficult to find that mental and muscular process that enables us to soften our eyes, then look upon a newborn baby. Our eyes soften and our hearts moisten, and our appreciation of Jesus' incarnation increases even more.

Murray Bowen developed an eightfold analysis of emotional processes as the foundation for family systems theory. Anxiety is one of the most potent drivers of these emotional processes. Bowen also applied his analysis to a societal level, outlining how 'The emotional system governs behavior on a societal level, promoting both progressive and regressive periods in a society ... In a regression, people act to relieve the anxiety of the moment rather than act on principle and a long-term view.'[19] Bowen, writing in the 1970s and 1980s is quite specific about the features of such regression:

> A regressive pattern began unfolding in society after World War II. It worsened some during the 1950s and rapidly intensified during the 1960s. The 'symptoms' of societal regression include a growth of crime and violence, an increasing divorce rate, a more litigious attitude, a greater polarization between racial groups, less principled decision-making by leaders, the drug abuse epidemic, an increase in bankruptcy, and a focus on rights over responsibilities.[20]

Bowen was remarkably prescient with this analysis, and he was bold in locating his analysis within the whole history of human society:

> Human societies undergo periods of regression and progression in their history. The current regression seems related to factors such as the population explosion, a sense of diminishing frontiers, and the depletion of natural resources. Bowen predicted that the current regression would, like a family in a regression, continue until the repercussions stemming from taking the easy way out on tough issues exceeded the pain associated with acting on a long-term view.

Bowen predicted 'that will occur before the middle of the twenty-first century and should result in human beings living in more harmony with nature'.[21] One is tempted to say, 'Well, that's all right

---

19 From Bowen Center for the Study of the Family <http://www.thebowen-center.org/ pages/conceptsep.html>.

20 Ibid.

21 Ibid.

then.' A dystopian perspective will not last forever, soon hopefulness will return, all we have to do is be patient. The challenge, if we follow Bowen's line, is what to do in the grim meantime?

There clearly are things to be done, but there is one thing in particular, and it comes in the shape of a most delightful aspect of the economy of abundance. Instead of anxiety being reduced by extensive self and group analysis and intensive heart-searching, anxiety can be lifted by fun and laughter. It was Peter Berger in his seminal book *The Sacred Canopy* who first coined the wonderful idea that laughter was like a rumour of angels. He, along with Harvey Cox in his book *The Feast of Fools*, recognised the mysterious role of laughter and playfulness. Interestingly, both Berger and Cox are concerned with the sociology of religion rather than theology per se. Social scientists have picked up the significance of laughter and humour, because they are distinctly human capacities, although research is now challenging this assumption.[22] The complex social world of Homo sapiens has fostered within the species the capacity for laughter and play to match our other distinctly human capacity, the capacity for worry and anxiety, that 'Sickness Unto Death' that Kierkegaard describes so graphically. Laughter and play are remarkable for their capacity to dissipate worry and anxiety, and for this reason laughter and play have survival value for the anxious species Homo sapiens. Play and laughter, combined with prayer and singing, are the most effective antidotes to anxiety, helping to shift us from the reptile brain that so easily fizzes with anxiety and is the locus of cold-blooded behaviour.

Whilst it might be stretching it to associate prayer with laughter, it is both legitimate and helpful to map the parallels between prayer and play. Both are acts of 'disciplined fantasy or ordered

---

22 I speculate that whales and dolphins might also go in for the occasional chuckle. Why? Because the females of these large sea mammals are the only other species in addition to Homo sapiens that experience a menopause. Biologists speculate that the reason why we and the whales invest in barren females is that the social environment in which offspring are reared is so complex that it cannot be mediated solely by the parent. Whales, dolphins and human beings all need their grannies, because grannies have the capacity to see the world from a nuanced, 'tongue-in-cheek' perspective.

imagination' and involve yielding 'to a kind of magic' to use terms coined by Hugo Rahner in his book *Man at Play*.[23] Neither prayer nor play is restricted by the mundane world of fact, they both go beyond it, and in doing so they pre-empt the future. In both playing and praying we assert that we are not beholden to past or present realities. Play and prayer enable us to step outside ideas of fate and fact, and allow us to start again; they are not an escape from or denial of the world, but rather the first steps in a dance of recreation.

If laughter and play are so important to the flourishing of humankind, the question has to be asked, why theologians have been so slow to give value to this rumour of angels? Perhaps it is because theology has been co-opted by the powerful throughout our Christendom history, because one of the most effective ways of undermining power is to turn it into a laughing stock. This is the tactic that is so precious to Community Organising – a movement based on the ideas of Saul Alinski which has been harnessed, particularly by the Catholic Church in the USA, and in Chicago – providing the young Barack Obama with his first job as a community organiser. Community Organising is now impacting on churches and communities in Britain, and here too is the recognition that if people can laugh at and joke about the things which have power over them, and oppress them, then they have embarked on a route to freedom.

Our church history is spotted with glimpses of comedy: from the medieval mummers and grotesque gargoyles to the occasional depiction of Christ as a clown or jester. Christ the clown, the man of sorrows who also wears a fool's cap, is an extraordinary symbol of both fun and seriousness. The idea of the clown is not just about humour, it also represents a perspective on life. The clown refuses to be limited to normal reality, fighting against the law of gravity, ridiculing the pompous, turning authority into a laughing stock, upsetting everyday rules and responsibilities. The clown is constantly defeated and trampled on, he is forever vulnerable, but never finally defeated; hope always remains a possibility. And the same might be said of Jesus. Our dismaying, anxious world is in need of jesters – jesters that enable us to laugh at our failures,

---

23 H. Rahner, *Man at Play*, English trans., London: Burns and Oates, 1965 p. 65.

prompt self-forgetfulness and encourage us to get up again, dust ourselves down and start all over again. However, if laughter is a rumour of angels, then perhaps laughter is like making the sign of the cross, because laughter can be a voice of faith, for it expresses an ironic confidence and joy, which may have no basis in fact, but is nonetheless real.

Dante, in the *Divine Comedy*, when he finally arrives in Paradise after all his trials and tribulations, hears the laughter of angels *praising* the Trinity. According to Dante, in Hell there is no hope and no laughter, in Purgatory there is hope but no laughter, but in Heaven there is no need of hope, so laughter reigns. Laughter is hope's last word.

5 It's Being So Cheerful that Keeps Us Going …[1]

Happy Days are here again
The skies above are clear again
Let us sing a song of cheer again
Happy days are here again.

So go the lines of Jack Yellen's popular song written in 1929. The cheeriness of the song was in keeping with the 'roaring twenties', a period, especially in the USA, characterised by creativity in music and art and soaring economic development; the good times rolled. Except that 1929 was also the year of the Great Wall Street Crash, which triggered the deep economic depression that ran through the 1930s, and which some say was only lifted by the mobilisation for World War II.

In 2008, the year when the banks went bust, there was likewise an escapist musical offering. The film *Mama Mia* was the most successful movie of the year. This reprise of Abba hits includes the number 'Money, Money, Money', which tells of the intention of a girl to find herself a wealthy man. 'Money, money, money always sunny … all the things I could do if I had a little money… it's a rich man's world … money, money, money must be funny in a rich man's world.' It is almost impossible to resist singing along.

One of the most fraudulent narratives that has infused our world is that money and happiness go together. Get money; spend

---

1   The colloquialism 'It's being so cheerful that keeps us going' has some truth to it. Researchers are intrigued by the findings that cheerfulness adds years to longevity of nuns. See M.E.P Seligman, *Authentic Happiness*, New York: Simon & Schuster Adult Publishing Group, 2002. A major research project looking at the life outcomes of nuns in the USA has been undertaken by David Snowden: see David Snowden, *Aging with Grace: What the Nun Study Teaches Us About Leading Longer, Healthier, and More Meaningful Lives*, New York: Bantam Books, 2001.

money; get possessions (or to use the new expression, 'get stuff'); become secure; relax and enjoy. This has been the implicit life plan that has dominated our lives for more than a century; it is a five-act play of seduction. And now, just as governments around the world want us to 'get stuff 'at a faster rate than ever, in order to give a helping hand to faltering economic growth, the link between wealth and stuff and well-being has been exposed as a fiction. The cat is out of the bag: once you can meet the cost of accommodation, clothing and food, then more money adds only a little to one's well-being. Liz Hoggard, on the basis of her work on the television programme *Making Slough Happy*, comments that, 'Wealth is like health: its absence breeds misery, but having it doesn't guarantee happiness.' And she goes on to say, 'Chasing money rather than meaning in life is a formula for discontent.'[2]

The growing amount of research into well-being has a positive impact on the movement through the J-Curve because the research repeatedly finds that having a sense of purpose and meaning in one's life is a big, big plus, and furthermore, this is strongly associated with taking one's faith seriously and engaging in religious practice. It is quite hard for a fiercely secular public arena and media-driven culture to acknowledge just how strongly faith figures in the recipe for well-being. Those who urge that God should be eliminated from our thinking, because of lack of evidence that God exists, have a struggle accommodating the mounting evidence that faith seems to be good for people. However, for people of faith it is a timely boost. When so much in the press either explicitly or implicitly demeans religious believers, it gives a positive fillip to read a headline in the *Daily Telegraph* that 'Church-goers Reap Healthy Reward',[3] or to discover that the Prime Minister's Strategy Unit, when working on the report 'Life Satisfaction: The State of Knowledge and Implications for Government', was faced with acknowledging evidence from the USA that going to church twice

2   L. Hoggard, *How to be Happy*, London: BBC Books, 2005, p. 64.
3   *The Daily Telegraph*, 11 August 1998, Roger Highfield, science editor, reporting on the research of Harold Koenig at Duke University that showed a significant difference in blood pressure amongst church attenders – to the benefit of church attenders, especially for African-Americans.

a week improves people's well-being equivalent to their salary being doubled.[4]

One of the earliest research programmes to uncover the significance of an active faith was undertaken by Blazer and Palmore.[5] More than thirty years ago they published research involving a 'longitudinal panel' of older people. For fifteen years they had researched a sample of older people as they aged and faced many of the challenges associated with old age. Blazer and Palmore wanted to identify the factors that were linked, not just with psychological well-being, but with retaining a sense of usefulness, and adjusting to the limitations associated with old age. Might it be having a healthy bank balance? Might it be having a spouse alive? Might it be having people who would regularly pop in? Or might the education level of the person have an impact? As well as investigating these variables, Blazer and Palmore were imaginative enough to explore the extent to which people had an active faith, and yes, you've got it: the factor that had by far the most significant positive impact on the experience of growing older was the extent to which people put their hand in the hand of God.[6]

In *The Challenge of Making Slough Happy* undertaken by Liz Hoggard and her team of experts, they too had to take into account the significance of religion to good mental health. Perhaps my perception is jaundiced, but despite clear evidence of the positive impact of faith, Hoggard's aim seems to be to 'reduce' faith to some other obviously healthy dynamic as she steers through the research:

---

4   'Life Satisfaction: The State of Knowledge and Implications for Government', the Prime Minister's Strategy Unit Dec. 2002, p. 26. This paper is to be found at <http://www.cabinetoffice.gov.uk/strategy/seminars/life_satisfaction.aspx>. The authors of the report (Nick Donovan and David Halpern with Richard Sargeant) give a rather loose citation for this research: 'Cited in "Social Capital, the Economy and Wellbeing" by John Helliwell, University of British Columbia (2001).' In my opinion, Donovan et al. are also less than thorough in drawing conclusions from their review of the literature on well-being, concluding that an increase in gardening would be a significant way of improving well-being. Which it would, but that is to tell only part of the story about well-being.

5   D. Blazer and E. Palmore, 'Religion and Aging in a Longitudinal Panel', *The Gerontologist*, vol. 16, no. 1 (1976).

6   Interestingly, the factor that had the second most positive effect on the experience of ageing was having someone who popped in regularly.

- So 'Maybe it's the social life'[7] because religion connects like-minded people together? Hoggard refers to Norenzayan, a Canadian psychologist who suggests that it is the social networking that happens in churches that helps reduce people's isolation, especially for the poor, the ill, the uneducated, the unmarried, the elderly and ethnic minorities. However, despite this reductive effort, Hoggard reluctantly has to conclude, 'However, researchers have found that people who attend church for non-spiritual reasons, such as wanting to make friends or gain in social importance, tend to have poorer mental health than those who go primarily because of their faith. This suggests that faith is necessary for the benefits to be felt.'[8]
- So, in explaining the evidence that 'Religion keeps you healthy,'[9] for example evidence that high levels of spirituality are associated with slower progression of illnesses such as Alzheimer's and other dementias,[10] Hoggard suggests that spirituality (when the research actually highlights the role of prayer), seems to enable the brain, through the neuro-endocrine system, to have positive effects on health. In passing, Hoggard also notes that those who take their faith seriously are less likely to be involved in self-destructive activities such as drug taking and alcohol abuse, and are less likely to divorce, which is a high source of stress and unhappiness.
- 'Religion saves people having to think for themselves.' This is not quite Hoggard's final insult. She notes the work of Barry Schwartz, who believes that one of the benefits of religious observance is that it frees people from having to make decisions for themselves.[11] The idea is that religious people can simply

---

7   Hoggard, p. 191.
8   Ibid., p. 192 .Hoggard does not provide references to this research.
9   Ibid., p. 194.
10   'We learned that the patients with higher levels of spirituality or higher levels of religiosity may have a significantly slower progression of cognitive decline,' said study author Yakir Kaufman, MD, who conducted the research as a fellow at of the Baycrest Centre for Geriatric Care in Toronto, Ontario and is now the director of neurology services at the Sarah Herzog Memorial Hospital in Jerusalem, Israel. *Science Daily*, 1 May 2005.
11   Barry Schwartz writes on the theme of the tyranny of choice in the modern world. Hoggard does not give any reference to Schwartz's research from which she draws her conclusion, but it may be from

follow the religion's teaching and thus avoid difficult debate.[12] The final insult that Hoggard dishes out is to return to Norenzayan's research to enable her to conclude that the links 'between religion, violence and intolerance are disturbing, with the more intense a person's religious commitment, the more intolerant they are towards others who think or behave differently ... (this) points towards the present day connection between religion and terrorism, ... and religious people are more likely to support wars.'[13]

I have focused on Hoggard's work because of its popularist nature. It is written for a wide, general audience, and its treatment of faith I consider to be unfair, but each and every author has the right to flaunt their prejudices.[14] When in the dip of the J-Curve it is tempting to grasp at all kinds of possibilities, and in particular for Christians to seize upon the mounting research that points to the positive gains that come from an active faith. But Hoggard demonstrates the ease with which such research results can be shaped and misrepresented. It is almost a cliché to wind up with the phrase attributed to Disraeli, 'There are three kinds of lies: lies, damned lies, and statistics.'

There is also another hazard, and Hoggard alludes to it. When we embrace faith because of what it will bring us, it is likely to bring us nothing at all. Just like happiness, faith, when it is pursued for

---

'Forming a New Congregation: The Uneasy Tension between Freedom and Community', *The Reconstructionist*, vol. 60, Spring (1995), pp. 48–56.

12   Hoggard, p. 192.

13   Ibid, p. 193. This use of Norenzayan's work seems to be careless or mischievous, in that the research conducted by Norenzayan finds that the more prayerful the person the less likely they are to scapegoat and to blame. For more on this see Ian Hansen and Ara Norenzayan, 'Between Yang and Yin and Heaven and Hell: Relationship Between Religion and Intolerance', in P. McNamara (ed.), *Where God and Science Meet*, Westport, CT: Greenwood Press, 2005.

14   One of the reasons why I make this accusation of bias is that Hoggard had to hand the following information: 'Of the dozens of studies that have looked at religion and happiness, the vast majority have found a positive link. Harold Koenig of Duke University Medical Center ... uncovered 100 papers on the subject, 79 of which showed that people who get involved in religion are happier or more satisfied with their lives, or have more positive emotions than others' (Hoggard, p. 216). This information Hoggard relegates to a footnote.

its functional benefit, depreciates into something less than faith. Like happiness, which cannot be pursued head-on without it deteriorating into hedonism, our Christian faith is *sui generis*, meaning that it stands in its own right, not to be reduced to a 'function' or a means to an end, or a product of something else. However, whilst this is an easy distinction to make in theory, in practice it is more complex. For example, the US Government under the direction of George W. Bush, provided funding to churches in recognition that Christian teaching and working for individual conversions, were key factors in achieving the transformation of long-term distressed communities. This is because the church is one of the few agencies that can achieve the 're-norming' of a community around the values of honesty, reciprocity and welcoming of the stranger.[15]

Research confirms that involvement in a church can enable people to 'get ahead', despite having faced long-term social deprivation. For example, involvement in a religious group is the best predictor of gaining employment. There is also growing evidence of the effectiveness of local churches in counteracting aggressive drug culture in their communities.[16] Speaking of the churches in New York City, community developer Van Johnson believes that there is no substitute for the resources of energy, enthusiasm, political clout and economic pull that churches offer to community developers. 'I will never again attempt to help people with economic revitalisation, unless it is under the umbrella of a church. It makes no sense, especially in the black community, to leave the church out. The church is the most important institution we have. It holds most of the resources that our community needs.'[17] This recognition of the importance of churches and the faith that they promote, to both

---

15   See F. Fukuyama, *The Great Disruption*, New York, Simon and Schuster, 1999, pp. 277–82.

16   See, for example, R. Carle, 'Church-Based Community Development and the Transformation of New York', *Trinity News*, vol. 44, no. 1 (1997), p. 14; L.R. Gruner, 'Heroin, Hashish, and Hallelujah: The Search for Meaning', *Review of Religious Research*, vol. 26, no.2, December (1984), pp. 176–84; C. Steinbach, 'Program Helps Restore Ailing Community', *Progressions*, vol. 5, no. 1, February (1995), p. 21; R.D. Carle and L.D. Decaro (eds), *Signs of Hope in the City*, Valley Forge, Judson Press.

17   Quoted in D. Wilson, 'Black Church Expands Communitarian Tradition', *Progressions*, vol. 5, no. 1, February (1995), p. 17.

well-being and social capital, presents a dilemma for policy makers and opinion formers.

For the past half-century, religious faith has been tolerated as a 'private good', but in contrast to the USA, in Britain there has been resistance to the recognition of 'faith' per se as a 'public good'. This is why churches can receive public monies to enable them to provide help and assistance to the vulnerable, but on condition that they must resist proselytising or encouraging people to develop confidence in God in the process of offering such help and support. The growing dilemma for policy makers and funding agencies is that research findings repeatedly point to the significance of a personal faith, or 'belief in something larger than oneself', in relation to increases in well-being and resilience. But nevertheless, in Britain teaching people about the Christian faith, and encouraging people to draw on the resource of faith, is off limits when public and increasingly charitable monies are involved.

The challenge to policy makers and funders becomes even more intense when the focus shifts from well-being and happiness to that of resilience. Happiness, especially, can be a rather flimsy and escapist idea, inviting recollection of the myriad times when we have heard or expressed the desire 'I just want to be happy.' In contrast, the idea of resilience carries a tough earthiness and the capacity to bounce back from setbacks. It is this tougher concept that has become greatly prized by those seeking to develop effective social policy and here, too, the policy makers wedded to secular approaches face a dilemma. In relation to resilience, I cite only three examples[18] of the research evidence that supports the role of faith as a positive resource:

- Bonnie Bernard, in the 1990s, identified religious commitment and a 'stable belief system' as significant factors in the ability of children to adapt well in the face of adversity.[19]
- Unaiza Niaz studied the contribution of faith (Islamic) to victims of the devastating earthquake that hit north-west Pakistan in

---

18 For those who can't get enough of this kind of material, I suggest you keep tabs on the Doxa Website at <http://www.doxa.ws/> and <www.authentichappiness.org>.

19 B. Bernard, *Fostering Resiliency in Kids: Protective Factors in the Family, School, and Community*, Portland, OR: Northwest Regional Educational Laboratory (ERIC Abstract), August 1991.

October 2005. She comments, 'Even in the face of such trauma and adversity, their sense of gratefulness and gratitude to God was overwhelming and inspiring. Instead of becoming resentful or loosing hope, they had sought refuge with God, religion and faith, asking him for help and at the same time thankful to him for being alive ... it is this very belief in God, faith in religion and prayer that has given the victims of earthquake [sic] the resilience that is not only vital for their survival through a time like this but also crucial to help them bounce back and establish themselves as before the calamity.'[20]

- C.S. Alcorta studied the protecting factors in relation to suicide amongst young people. Her work demonstrated that 'not all adolescents subjected to risk factors develop depression. Accumulating research suggests that one factor that may contribute to adolescent resilience is religious involvement ... this study identified specific elements of religious involvement that contribute to adolescent resilience by enhancing social skills, expanding problem solving strategies, and increasing positive effect (wellbeing).'[21]

WARNING: TRICKY TERRAIN AHEAD!

It is reassuring that a growing body of research links religious behaviour with resilience and other 'social goods'. Marketing executives would rejoice at such evidence to support the efficacy of their product and it is tempting to rejoice likewise. Surely such objective evidence will prosper our churches and enable sturdy growth, and the doldrums will be left behind? Alleluia! We are out of the dip! Well maybe, but caution is needed. In addition to the meagre and even dishonourable reference that the media are likely to give to research findings that highlight the benefit of religious commitment, the reality is that the interpretation of research findings is far from straightforward. Research design and analysis are fraught with complexity, and prone to both unintended and

---

20   U. Niaz, 'Role of Faith and Resilience in Recovery from Psychotrauma', *Pakistani Journal of Medical Science*, vol. 22, no. 2 (2006), pp. 204–207.
21   C.S. Alcorta, 'Youth, Religion and Resilience', PhD thesis (December 2006), abstract available at <http://proquest.umi.com>.

subtly intended bias. For every encouragement to be found in the growing number of research findings that are supportive of the role of faith, there will be a counter-argument, to the extent that debate becomes characterised not by insight but by petty dispute.

There are other reasons to be alert to the potential distraction that these apparently encouraging research findings offer. In chapter 4 I drew attention to the economy of abundance that Jesus encourages us to embrace, and the research that is emerging supports the reality of this alternative economy, demonstrating how faith can be a foundational, positive life force. However, the manner in which this encouraging development is taken up is prone to the tactics that belong to the economy of scarcity. In the previous chapter I drew on the work of Zander and Zander to highlight some of the aptitudes that we develop if our view of the world is dominated by the idea of scarcity and peril. These skills were things like developing a clever strategic mind, assessing strength and weakness, resisting challenges to our own point of view and investing in our self-interest and the interests of our clan.[22] By investing too much in these encouraging research findings we risk honing these very aptitudes and approaches that have been fostered by the fight–flight inclination of our animal nature, rather than practising the ways in which Jesus showed us how to live.

There is a further caution about using this growing research culture as an expression of enacted hope. From Luke's Gospel we find Jesus expressing a woe: 'Woe to you when all men speak well of you, for that is how their fathers treated the false prophets.'[23] Another stern warning is to be found in Luke 16:14–15 'The Pharisees ... were sneering at Jesus. He said to them, "You are the ones who justify yourselves in the eyes of men, but God knows your hearts. What is highly valued among men is detestable in God's sight"' (NIV). These verses are almost too convenient in their application to this emerging context where religious faith and religious agencies can be viewed as health-giving and vital to well-being and resilience, the very 'products' that are prized by policy makers.

---

22 These items are informed by R.S. Zander and B. Zander, *The Art of Possibility*, London: Penguin, 2000, especially the chapter 'Stepping into a Universe of Possibility', pp. 17–23.

23 Luke 6:26 NIV.

For those who work for the well-being of the poor and disparaged, these verses from Luke's Gospel make for a quandary. When there is evidence that faithful practice does indeed enact hope in people who are locked in struggle, it would be perverse not to harness this capacity, and to seek all the resources possible to deliver this capacity ever more effectively and extensively. To achieve this means that those with funds to disburse need to think well of you. The funding applications that need to be drafted have to promote and even boast of the exceptional outcomes that faith groups can achieve. It is here that reflectiveness becomes an essential ingredient if the pitfalls expressed in Luke's Gospel are to be avoided. There are three issues on which it is useful to reflect:

- There is a common-sense view that if something is useful or effective it is assumed that it must be a good thing. This is a version of 'functionalism' which values things as a 'means to an end', rather than valuing them for their own sake. Functionalism is essentially a secularising force, in that it reduces everything to its earthly effect and reduces everything to the service of 'man'. Therefore, functionalism, as an approach, values our Christian faith and practice because they work as a transformational dynamic. But this reduces the nature of faith to what it *can do*, rather than allowing faith to have validity in its own right. This is the *sui generis* issue that was raised earlier and so often accompanies debate about religion. For those who take faith seriously, and as the focus or heart of our lives, faith is *sui generis*, i.e. faith is a distinctive phenomenon, valid in its own right and irreducible, and therefore not to be treated as being (really) about something else.
- The *via negativa* is part of classical Christian tradition.[24] Thomas Aquinas commends the *via negativa* as one of the ways we can work to develop holiness and discipleship. The *via negativa* is the discipline of remembering that 'this is not it'. It

---

24 The notion of the *via negativa* is also present in other religions, for example *neti neti* in Hinduism, *ein-sof* in Judaism and *bila faifa* in Islam, and there are pages and pages that could be written as to how the 'this is not it' emphasis at the heart of the *via negativa* is a means of spiritual development for the Buddhist. Interestingly, the 'negative way' has also been taken up by postmodern thinkers such as Derrida and De Certeau.

is the refusal to allow any response to be thought of, or treated as, the final or complete response. For those committed to working for justice and peace in troubled neighbourhoods, and therefore wanting and needing to promote the resources of faith and religious practice, the discipline of the *via negativa* can bring protection from potential hazards. The *via negativa* gives motivation to keep alert and open to the new, and urges the imagination onward. It provides a reminder of the need for continual humility. The honest embrace of the *via negativa* can also provide an antidote to the accumulation of status and power that tempts us to trade in the economy of scarcity.

• And *realpolitik*: government policies throughout Britain are focusing on local delivery and decision making. However, the theologian William Cavanaugh highlights the danger of the State undermining what happens at local level. National government both consciously and unconsciously can usurp, co-opt and exclude local civil society, excluding other approaches and ways of seeing things, i.e. undermining other *discourses* or centres of authority. Cavanaugh suggests that the modern nation state, despite its best intentions, habitually steals power from lesser communal bodies[25] by narrowing the imagination and range of responses that are made by people at local level.

It would be wrong to ignore the growing research evidence that highlights the positive impact of faith and religious practice on individuals and neighbourhoods. Whilst there may be hazards, this research evidence is also confirmation of the viability and obliqueness of the economy of abundance, in which Jesus coaches us through the way in which he lived his life. So what is going on? How is it that faith and religious practice can be so transformational, especially when people are in hard situations? There are some clues and it is in relation to the way we make sense of our *circumstances* that it is critical – and therefore very relevant to the troubled times that make us bothered and bewildered.

---

25 W. Cavanaugh, *Theopolitical Imagination*, Edinburgh: T & T Clark, 2002, p. 72.

A MATTER OF CIRCUMSTANCE

Richard Layard, the economist who has pioneered work on well-being and wealth,[26] makes a case that is almost shocking in its simplicity: increasing the income of those who are poor, both in the UK and overseas, is more effective in promoting the *well-being of everyone* than increasing the income of the rich, because even for those who are only moderately financially secure, more money brings disappointment. What is going on here is to do with the mysterious terrain of 'circumstances'. *Circumstances* are a taken-for-granted but often misapprehended dynamic in our lives. Our circumstances are an amalgam of the time, the place, the environment, and the past events that impact on each of us. The assumption is that this cocktail is a powerful factor influencing the way we see life and the choices we make in our life.

It is this business of 'circumstances' that diminishes the impact of money on well-being. Layard's analysis highlights 'habituation' (which means we quickly get used to our circumstances), as one of the reasons why the anticipated delight associated with high earnings or a windfall dulls quite quickly. Basically we get used to what we have and the lifestyle associated with wealth becomes routine. The second factor that Layard identifies is that of status anxiety. We cannot resist comparing our circumstances with others: rivalry is hard to resist. So, rather than relax in financial security, we find ourselves having to negotiate a new batch of worries about losing out on the advantages that others have secured. Here we have an echo of Girard's work on the 'mimetic of desire'. In other words, we rarely assess our circumstances objectively, but rather we assess them in comparison with others.

The work of positive psychologists suggests that circumstances matter, but not as much as we think. There is an inclination to cede too much potency to 'circumstances' in making sense of our lives; 'circumstances' have acquired a more potent status in our life script than is warranted. Positive psychology, which has been energised by the work of Martin Seligman,[27] is based on research that suggests we are inclined to overestimate the impact of circumstances on our

---

26 R. Layard, *Happiness: Lessons from a New Science*, London: Allen Lane, 2005.
27 M. Seligman founded the field of positive psychology in 2000. He directs the Positive Psychology Center at the University of Pennsylvania.

lives and *underestimate* the scope we have for 'intentional activity'. There are three things that have been identified as having an impact on well-being:

- circumstances
- our 'set-point'
- intentional activity.

Circumstances 10%

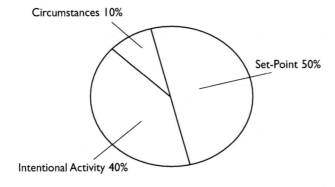

Set-Point 50%

Intentional Activity 40%

Figure 5.1
Source: Lyubomirsky, Sheldon and Schkade[28]

The set-point comes from our genes. Our genes play a significant part in whether we are upbeat or prone to gloom. This doesn't mean that those with gloomy genes can never be happy, just that when they are happy the gloomy genes are prone to pull them back to our 'set-point'. But this is only half of the story. The surprise is how little impact 'circumstances' have on people's well-being. Research suggests just 10 per cent. If we can get the motivation to engage in positive or meaningful intentional activities, circumstances associated with our health, money and even upbringing have a surprisingly small impact on well-being. So lottery winners are no happier one year after their win, and at the other end of the scale, people with paralysis are often not as unhappy as might be expected.[29] This research also supports

28 S. Lyubomirsky, K.M. Sheldon and D. Schkade (2005) 'Pursuing Happiness: The Architecture of Sustainable Change,' Review of General Psychology, Special Issue: Positive Psychology 9 (2005), pp. 111–131.

29 See the work of A. Oswald and N. Pawdthavee, *Does Happiness Adapt? A Longitudinal Study of Disability with Implications for Economists and Judges*, mimeo, University of Warwick, September 2005.

Layard's observation that people 'habituate' or rapidly adapt to new circumstances, and return to their baseline emotional level, i.e. to their set-point.

This idea that circumstances have such a small impact on well-being is counter-intuitive, and equally, it is hard to believe that there is so much scope for intentional activity to have a positive impact. (Although, the two are closely related because previous intentional activity shapes and informs current circumstances.) Our inclination to overestimate the degree to which we are limited by circumstances may be due to what psychologists refer to as 'the focusing illusion', i.e. 'Nothing in life is quite as important as you think it is while you are thinking about it.'[30] Furthermore, because our circumstances have a major impact on the way in which we engage with the market, i.e. our ability to buy stuff, it follows that the part that circumstances play in relation to well-being gets over-valued. In other words, in falling for the illusion that wealth and well-being go hand in hand, we also fall into the trap of overesti-mating the impact of circumstances on our life.

This simple three-part model of genes, circumstances and inten-tional activity is dynamite. It scuppers the long-standing dilemma

---

30   'The focusing illusion helps explain why the results of well-being research are often counter-intuitive. The false intuitions may arise from a failure to recognize that people do not continuously think about their circum-stances, whether positive or negative – Nothing in life is quite as important as you think it is while you are thinking about it. Individuals who have recently experienced a significant life change (e.g. becoming disabled, winning a lottery, or getting married) surely think of their new circum-stances many times each day, but the allocation of attention eventually changes, so that they spend most of their time attending to and drawing pleasure or displeasure from experiences such as having breakfast or watching television ... For example an experiment in which students were asked: (i) 'How happy are you with your life in general?' and (ii) 'How many dates did you have last month?' The correlation between the answers to these questions was –0.012 (not statistically different from 0) but when they were asked in the reverse order, the correlation rose to 0.66 with another sample of students. [By asking] The dating question [first, this] evidently caused that aspect of life to become salient and its importance to be exaggerated when the respondents encountered the more general question about their happiness', D. Kahneman, A.B. Krueger, D. Schkade et al., 'Would You be Happier if You Were Richer? A Focusing Illusion', *Science*, vol. 312 (2008), pp. 1908–10 <http://www.sciencemag.org/cgi/content/abstract/312/5782/1908>.

at the heart of the social sciences: that man makes society, and society makes man, restoring to people the capacity to act with some autonomy. It challenges the helping professions to examine the extent to which their practice helps people embrace the scope for meaningful intentional activity, rather than reinforcing or further pathologising the dire aspects of their circumstances. It enlarges our understanding of poverty to include character, i.e. the sense of personal agency and responsibility, combined with a capacity to hold off the desire for immediate gratification. It also puts the spotlight on wealth, which, in a world that has been duped into thinking that wealth brings the things that really matter, continues to give an unwarranted influence and status.

The growing canon of research into well-being suggests that the wealthy need to develop character more than they might expect, if they are to live life in all its fullness. Perhaps it was this that Jesus was alluding to when talking with the rich young man. In refusing to accept the limitations associated with our circumstances, and taking hold of the scope for meaningful intentional behaviour, we move into the politically charged territory of character. Richard Reeves, the director of the left-leaning think-tank Demos, comments in relation to character: 'It is a treacherous political terrain, but one in which governments are increasingly entangled. Anyone who is interested in creating a successful liberal society is interested in character too, whether they admit it or not. Good societies need good people.'[31]

This potent model suggests we are inclined to over-rate the impact of circumstances and underestimate the significance of our 'agency' (i.e. our ability to engage in meaningful intentional activities), and it is this that helps to account for the effectiveness of religious commitment and practice in initiating and sustaining change in people's lives. The commitment to follow Jesus in the way he lived his life is a major contributor to empowerment which enables a sense of purpose to flourish. Embracing commitment to follow Jesus impacts on our attitude to our circumstances, and when our attitudes change so too do the micro-actions in which we engage. Layard quotes Victor Frankl, who concluded from his experiences in Auschwitz that in the last resort 'everything can be

---

31   R. Reeves, 'A Question of Character', *Prospect*, August (2008).

taken from a man but one thing, the last of human freedoms – to choose one's attitude in any given set of circumstances'. [32] Becoming a Christian is about making an effort to choose one's attitude to one's circumstances.

Intentional behaviour can be good or bad or insignificant, it can be an expression of alienation or anomie, or it can be directed towards pleasure seeking or philanthropy – and over time it adds accretions to our circumstances. In order to help people take full advantage of the scope for intentional behaviour to improve well-being, positive psychology focuses on attitudes, and the attitude which is given most attention is that of gratitude. Gratitude or gratefulness 'is a knowing awareness that we are recipients of goodness', so writes Robert Emmons. He goes on to note that an 'essential aspect of gratitude is the notion of *undeserved merit*'. [33] Here Emmons could be describing 'grace'. The significance of gratitude in opening us up to the scope for intentional behaviour is rooted in the process of acknowledging the gift or generosity that comes from others. This encourages us to look outside ourselves, and through this we begin to locate ourselves within an intricate pattern of relationships that grow stronger through the dynamics of mutuality and obligation.

For Christians, in response to God's generosity we respond with gratitude, because that is what we do in praising God. But for some, circumstances are such that gifts and generosity are rare, or circumstances so hard that gratitude seems impossible. Here, when alongside people confronted by harsh circumstances, the positive psychologists seem unembarrassed by drawing on religious practices. Emmons writes: 'The religious traditions encourage us to do more than react with passivity and resignation to a loss or crisis; they advise us to change our perspective, so that our suffering is transformed into an opportunity for growth.'[34] Emmons amplifies how this comes about: 'Religious traditions ... articulate visions of how we should respond to the fact that life is full of suffering ... People can adopt an attitude toward their suffering that

---

32 Cited by Layard, p. 8, taken from V. Frankl, *Man's Search for Meaning*, New York: Basic Books, 1985 (no page number given).

33 R. Emmons, *Thanks!*, New York: Houghton Mifflin, 2007, pp. 6–7. Italics in the original.

34 Ibid., p. 160.

allows it to be a meaningful component of life, perhaps opening the threshold to a deeper, more authentic existence.'[35] By allowing existence itself to be a gift and ourselves to be enfolded in the grace or generosity of God, especially in trying times, the commitment to keep praising God is to enact gratitude.

This recognition of the health-giving nature of gratitude goes some way to freeing the Christian faith from the accusation of being an opiate that stifles intentional behaviour. Karl Marx viewed Christianity as delaying the inevitable revolution by captivating the proletariat with a false consciousness that meant they embraced a Christian faith even though it was against their interests. As a tool of the ruling class, the opiate of religious faith both stupefied and induced inertia, and this line has been taken by many historians subsequently. And let's be frank, it is easy to see how encouraging people to practise gratitude and count blessings, naming them one by one, could easily be viewed as coaxing people to accept their unjust and inhuman conditions. And in some instances this might be a valid criticism, but not in all cases.

REVOLUTIONARY

The word 'revolution' needs to be used sparingly, for it is a rare historical state. In the context of this discussion about circumstances and the capacity to embrace the scope for intentional behaviour, then revolution is climactic. Revolution involves throwing off the perceived constraints of circumstance and taking up intentional activity both individually and corporately. It involves transformation of values and approaches, bringing new ways of seeing and a new way of organising, resulting in a shift in the balance of power away from the status quo. Many historians have consciously adopted a Marxist interpretation of history[36] and therefore viewed religion and religious practice as inhibitors of revolutionary change. However, as enchantment with Marxism has withered, other interpretations of the role of religion have come to the fore. In particular, historians have revisited the impact of Methodism and have begun

---

35 Ibid.
36 For example, E. Hobsbawn, E.P. Thompson, R. Challinor, G. Lefebvre; C.L.R. James, Philip Foner and the list could go on and on.

to acknowledge that Methodism and the Evangelical revival *was* a revolution in England,[37] and furthermore, the manner of this revolution meant that England was spared the violence that characterised the French Revolution.[38]

A case can be made that, rather than crushing the spirits of the new industrial proletariat, religious enthusiasm, and Methodism in particular:

> may have helped the working men to face the challenges of the burgeoning industrial order, and others have added, may even have prepared them for a later socialism. If the Hammonds (historians), for example, saw Wilberforce as a villain and Evangelicalism as an opiate, they were none the less prepared to grant that Methodism had made many men 'better rebels'.[39]

To be a good rebel involves the capacity to resist the norms and sanctions on one's behaviour; it is, like revolution, the epitome of shaking oneself free from circumstances and opting for intentional behaviour, and the suggestion is that Methodism accomplished this amongst 'the anxious – the dislocated, the rootless, the disturbed'[40] by preaching the message that, though there is nothing in us that merits God's goodness, God invites us to receive his grace.

Almost three hundred years later the echoes of this message of the life-giving significance of *undeserved merit* come to us from the positive psychologists. We are now able to have a more nuanced perspective on the practice of gratitude and the recognition and response to grace: it does not have to lead to domestication; it can also empower us to resist or even rebel against the power of circumstances. This is hugely relevant to our current inclination

---

37 B. Semmel in *The Methodist Revolution*, London Heinemann, 1973, suggests there are two reasons why historians have underestimated the transformational and revolutionary features of Methodism in particular: That historians have focused on Calvinist rather than Methodist theology and not gathered evidence regarding the local impact of Methodism. Semmel, 1973, p. 4.
38 This thesis is associated with Elie Halévy; see B. Semmel, *Elie Halévy, Methodism and Revolution*, Chicago: University of Chicago Press, 1971.
39 Semmel, 1973, p. 4. Semmel's reference to the Hammonds is to J.L. Hammond and B. Hammond, *The Town Labourer, 1760–1832*, London: Longmans Green, 1918, p. 287.
40 Ibid., p. 7.

towards a dystopian worldview. Circumstances must not be allowed to dictate the script and narrow down people's options. In claiming the rebellious slogan that 'life doesn't have to be like this', history and the social sciences increasingly support the idea that faith can provide the empowerment to cross the threshold into the open terrain of intentional behaviour.

There is one area where it is particularly difficult to step beyond circumstances and this is in relation to addictions. Just as the species Homo sapiens is an anxious species, so too are we an addictive species. It is in relation to addiction that intentional activity consolidates or fuses with our circumstances. Addiction saps our best intentions, closing the door on other possibilities for life. But again history points to the ability of faith and faith practices to help people break through the entrapping circumstances of addiction. In 1865, the Salvation Army was co-founded by William and Catherine Booth. William was a Methodist preacher, and together they took the notion of Wesleyan holiness to 'the submerged tenth'. The movement spread rapidly, and was perhaps one of the earliest 'popular' global movements. It was a bold and innovative movement, seeking to engage with the poorest and most broken, often broken by chronic alcohol abuse. The Salvation Army achieved what today seems impossible:[41] to invite those broken and damaged by circumstances into positions of responsibility and leadership, that is to become sufficiently free of addiction to be able to embrace intentional activity.

In our culture which is dismissive of hierarchy and resentful of authority, the firmly hierarchical practice of the Salvation Army is easy to write off. Even if it did succeed in helping people to get free of addiction to alcohol and grinding poverty, the Salvation Army is dismissed because this was achieved at the cost of personal freedom, as people were recruited as soldiers and embellished with many of the trappings of the military, including the requirement to obey senior members. But this is to ignore some outstanding achievements in relation to intentional activity. It may be apocryphal, but the witness of the woman who declares that 'I'd rather have my husband beat the Salvation Army drum than beat me!' is one of the early cries of the emancipation of women. Part of the rebellious spirit of the Salvation Army (in addition to the

---

41   It could be said that Alcoholics Anonymous achieve this today.

charges of 'vulgarity, levity and frivolity'[42]), was to encourage women as much as men into positions of leadership, and to do likewise in relation to those of African or Indian heritage. Whilst the Salvation Army might have modelled itself on a military chain of command, it also undermined the patriarchal power of the Victorian household,[43] and put into practice the Gospel teaching that we are all God's children, regardless of gender and ethnicity, a thoroughly rebellious notion in that period.

In this chapter I have tried to demonstrate how well-being has its roots in what in chapter 4 I referred to as the economy of abundance, rather than in the economy of scarcity. The awareness of what makes for a sense of well-being is essential in dystopian times. We are responsible as much for gloom as we are for cheerfulness. My aim has not been to harness the growing amount of research that links well-being with faith and religious practice, to jump start a journey up the right side of the J-Curve, although that is tempting. Rather, I have tried to use the insights from positive psychology to liberate the historic efforts of Methodism and Salvationism from the stereotype of dealing in the opiate of the people, subduing the capacity of the poor to open the door into revolutionary intentional activity.

What has been implied, rather than spelt out, is the significance of meaningfulness to sustained well-being, and meaningfulness requires a narrative of emancipation[44] that enables one to make sense of one's life within a hope-filled future. In a time when people are bothered and bewildered this is part of the new pastoral challenge for churches: to enable people to reflect on their circumstances and to weigh up whether the example of Jesus can provide a narrative of emancipation that enables people to make sense of their life within a meaningful and hope-filled future.

---

42 See V. Bailey, *In Darkest England and the Way Out: The Salvation Army, Social Reform and the Labour Movement 1885–1910, International Review of Social History*, vol. 29, no. 2 (1984).

43 See L. Marks, 'The Hallelujah Lasses: Working Class Women in the Salvation Army in English Canada 1882–92', in F. Iacovetta and M. Valverde (eds), *Gender Conflicts*, Toronto: University of Toronto Press, 1992, pp. 67–118.

44 François Lyotard used the term 'emancipation narrative' to describe a narrative that points to a redemptive future. F. Lyotard, *The Postmodern Condition: A Report on Knowledge*, 1979, trans. Geoff Bennington et al., Minneapolis: University of Minnesota Press, 1984.

6 Church for the Bothered and Bewildered

In a world that has gone gloomy and in which people are bothered and bewildered, there are new *pastoral* challenges for the church. There is the challenge of helping people get beyond anxiety-driven responses, and the pastoral challenge of helping people to reflect on their circumstances and to weigh up whether the example of Jesus can provide a way of making sense of their lives, within a hope-filled rather than dismal future. In the context of an ever more mission-shaped church, to emphasise the significance of pastoral care is rather old-fashioned, but, as Stephen Pattison suggests, the church in rampant 'missionary mode' needs more than ever to reconnect with pastoral responsibilities. He writes:

> If the Pastoral is cast as attending to and nurturing God's world, and all that is in it, for God's sake, then this is a mode of under-standing and acting that is essential, if mission is not to be about a rather crude preoccupation with a certain type of conversion and colonisation ... if pastoral care is one of the places were Christians learn who and what they are called to be, and thus what they need to do, then we relegate pastoral care to insignificance at our peril.[1]

Furthermore, the resource of pastoral care is vital in troubled times, when people can easily get bogged down by circumstances and fail to see the potential for different outcomes.

In troubled times, mission and pastoral care have to be allies. Pastoral care traditionally involves the helper harnessing their skills and sensitivity in order to help foster resilience in those beset

---

1   S. Pattison, 'Is Pastoral Care Dead in a Mission-Led Church?', *Practical Theology*, vol. 1, no. 1 (2008), pp. 7–10.

by challenges in their lives. This aim and approach is both valid and commendable in the anticipation of a dystopian future. Ravi Zacharius coined the phrase 'steadying the soul when the heart is under pressure', in his response to the events on 11 September 2001 in the USA. The year 2001 may well come to be seen as the watershed between a utopian worldview and the dystopian perspective. The change in our disposition was anticipated by Zacharius when he wrote, 'Our lifestyles will be changed because evil demands a response and the response agonizes the tender conscience of good people. We have not seen the end of pain. It is part of the cost of caring and loving.'[2] Zacharius has a knack of capturing the zeitgeist – the spirit of the times – and by unpicking his words it is possible to begin to spell out the new mood music of a dystopian worldview:

- By caring and loving, more than ever, we risk having our hearts broken – as much as finding fulfilment.
- Compassionate responses risk being judged as naiveté.
- Dismay and anxiety – rather than pleasure and optimism – characterise the outlook.
- We shall require the neglected practice of self-discipline if not to be imprisoned by our circumstances.

Furthermore, the new priorities that are called for by this sudden 'about-turn' from confidence in progress to a bothered and bewildered state, have to be addressed in the context of a fragmenting and anxious church culture. It is for this reason that reflective practice is essential. When we embrace reflective practice our church practice changes. Reflective practice in dismal times may mean that we stand before God with less confidence; such confidence becoming a gracious moment akin to a religious experience rather than a 'right'. Karl Barth's comment on the danger at the heart of sermonising highlights how our confidence in relation to God may become more humble. Barth comments, 'What are you

---

2   This paper is available at <http://www.rzim.org/resources/essay_arttext.php?id=6>, part of the website of Ravi Zacharius International Ministries.

doing, you man, with the word of *God* upon *your* lips? Upon what grounds do you assume the role of mediator between heaven and earth? Who has authorized you to take your place there and generate religious feeling?'[3] The answer is that in a fragmenting, irritable world, no authority, religious or otherwise, can grant such legitimacy. No longer are people convinced by the assumed virtue of institutional power. Authority has to be earned, based on the enacting or performing of hope, and this means that the focus has, for the most part, to be at local level, and both pastoral care and fresh expressions of the process of being church must have a role in this.

WATCH OUT FOR THE WORRIED MONIED

Ravi Zacharius' phrase 'steadying the soul when the heart is under pressure' can be extended in a bothered and bewildered world – steadying the soul when the heart *and head* are under pressure, because in a bothered and bewildered world, fear becomes endemic. In previous chapters I have given an account of the impact that anxiety has on our behaviour; fear is a notch further up on the panic scale. Jacques Ellul suggests that fear 'dictates two modes of behaviour: violence and rigidity'.[4] Pastoral care has, for the sake of everyone, to find ways of addressing palpable, contagious fear, and mission strategies have to take account of rigidity of belief. In particular, it is in relation to the *non-poor* that this alertness is needed. In the twentieth century it was the middle classes who sustained the fascist enterprises of Mussolini and Hitler.

The investment by the non-poor in personal competence, wealth, and expectation of positive recognition by employers comes under threat in dystopian times. There is an implicit theology that underpins these values and resulting lifestyle: *through our competence, reliability and contribution to the nation through our taxes, we foster well-being in society. Unlike the poor, who are a demand on the State and have not worked to better themselves, we are*

---

3   K. Barth, *The Word of God and the Word of Man*, New York: Harper and Row, 1957, p. 125. The italics are his.

4   J. Ellul, *Living Faith: Belief and Doubt in a Perilous World*, trans. P. Heinegg, New York: Harper and Row, 1980, p. 109.

educated and have invested in our careers and families. Through these commitments and values we pay homage to our God. In dystopian times these perspectives and sentiments come under pressure because employers are as much likely to dismiss as reward, blessings from the economy of scarcity (the market economy) have become scarcer, and the long-term reward of a pension has been eroded. When the crude theology that gives succour to 'proficiency and reward' (meritocracy) fails to deliver, then predictably, the unease that results generates the desire to blame and seek out scapegoats. In contrast to the non-poor, it is the poor who are most likely to have come to terms with the uncertainty, unfairness and vulnerability that can intrude daily into life, and still be able to praise God.[5] In dystopian times, those who have endured hardship longest are likely to those who can give clues about coping mechanisms and realistic theology.

Reflecting on the relevance of the story of Jesus, and then going on to try and practise it in one's life, is relevant to what is referred to as the *pastoral cycle*. The pastoral cycle aims at a continuous process of engagement with, and reflection upon, the world and the word of God, in order that a course of action can be discerned and acted upon with a view to bringing things closer to God's desire for his world.

The pastoral cycle enables the outcomes of an action (enacted hope) to be celebrated, evaluated and further reflected on in a continuing cycle. The commitment to continual re-evaluation at the heart of the pastoral cycle embodies the spiritual insight of the *via negativa* – the principle of 'this is not it' referred to in chapter 5 – and it is a tool rightly valued by Christian social activists. Most often, the pastoral cycle is used as a tool to shape and critique engagement in justice and peace by Christians; it is also an approach which enables theology to be 'contextualised'. These are undoubted virtues. However, in the troubled times that we now face, the emphasis of the pastoral cycle needs to include scrutiny of personal behaviour. This brings the pastoral cycle back to its roots in Kolb's Learning Cycle.[6]

---

5 It would be interesting to undertake research into the relationship that those who have endured long-term poverty have with their God. I have a hunch that God is very close, especially for women.

6 See D.A. Kolb, *Experiential Learning: Experience as a Source of Learning and Development*, New Jersey: Prentice Hall, 1984.

Kolb's Learning Cycle, like the pastoral cycle, has four stages:

1 Doing/having an experience (concrete experience).
2 Reviewing/reflecting on the experience (reflective observation).
3 Concluding/learning from the experience (abstract conceptualisation).
4 Planning/trying out what you have learned (active experimentation).

Kolb's cycle enables even the micro-actions that shape our daily encounters and decision making to be reflected upon. With the addition of reflecting on one's 'performance' from the perspective of the way Jesus lived and taught, this cycle resembles the intuitive practice of the class system of early Methodism and Salvationists. Hempton writes of the Methodist class: 'Classes were groups of about twelve meeting in a particular geographic area under a specified leader. Entry was based on the desire to "flee the wrath to come" and the aim was to nurture godly language, temperance, honesty, plainness, seriousness, frugality, diligence, charity, and economic loyalty within the connection.'[7]

NEW LESSONS TO LEARN

The class system of Methodism and the equivalent gathering of Salvationists was the way in which people were able to get beyond the limitations of their circumstance, and stretch for the extensive scope for positive and creative intentional activity (as explored in detail in chapter 5). The classes were an early manifestation of motivational workshops; they were both missional and pastoral, and hugely effective in terms of the impact on individuals and in terms of numeric growth. It would be naïve to imagine that 'classes' could be easily recreated two hundred years on, nor would the 'curriculum' be the same. However, they do provide a measuring rod against which to evaluate our prevailing processes of church, in the face of the pressing pastoral responsibility of *steadying the*

---

7 D. Hempton, *Methodism: Empire of the Spirit*, New Haven: Yale University Press, 2005, p. 78.

soul when the heart and head are under pressure. In order to be able to enact hope in dismal times, there are nine aptitudes that people need to develop:

1 To be a non-anxious presence in stressful times.
2 To practise systemic thinking in order to resist the temptation to blame others when things go wrong.
3 To practise gratitude – even in difficult circumstances.
4 To engage in courageous micro-actions that counter the inclination towards neo-tribalism and fragmentation rather than social cohesion (e.g. the *conversation* that Jesus has with the Samaritan woman at the well – see chapter 2).
5 To imagine ways of breaking out of the constraints of circumstances and have the motivation and discipline to persist with intentional behaviour.
6 To gain confidence in the viability of the economy of abundance and generosity that Jesus inducts us into, rather than being beholden to the economy of scarcity.
7 To practise sitting more lightly on the globe in recognition of our thoughtless abuse of the creation.
8 To practise compassion, conviviality and harness the imagination to ward off the dangers of gnosticism.
9 To draw on the enriching memories of eras past in order to affirm the human capacity to 'correct its own errors'[8] or in more theological language, 'to repent' or 'turn about'.

All of us need help to reflect on how to achieve these states of mind and the 'performance' that then follows. This requires attentive dialogue and a context of trust and solidarity, and this gives a major clue about the process of church that endeavours to enact hope in troubled times.

A further clue about the process of church in troubled times is a corollary of having confidence in abundance, echoing Julian of Norwich's sentiment that 'all shall be well and all manner of things shall be well'. When confident in the economy of abundance we care less about being in control and we take more risks. This

---

8   J. Sacks, *Celebrating Life*, London: Continuum, 2000, p. 173.

brings with it the capacity to let go of short-term advantage and commit to a longer perspective, where we are even less likely to be able to predict, let alone control, the outcome. Whilst in the economy of scarce resources we set a goal and pursue it, in contrast the process of church that is confident in a gracious, abundant economy will *embrace a context in a way that assumes hopeful possibility*. However, too often, our imagination falters in relation to the church, and like everyone else we assume that the accumulation of power and resources and the ability to control and direct things are the only things that are worthwhile. What are we to do if not to pursue success in terms of numbers, money in the coffers and building developments, and gain more and more vocations so that the influence and impact of 'church' can expand?

ASSUMING HOPEFUL POSSIBILITY

I offer three examples of what the process of church might look like when it 'embraces a context in a way that assumes hopeful possibility'. The first two examples demonstrate the capacity of a 'holy space' to empower people to face up to their circumstances (their context), and admit how close to defeat they might be, but also strengthen their motivation to embrace positive intentional activity.

There is a church that makes sure its doors are open every evening from half-past eight until ten o'clock. The doors are open for those who care about young people in that neighbourhood, particularly those youngsters who are caught up in drugs. Mums, grandparents and fathers come in and light a candle, and on occasion, in that holy space, sob for the sake of their children. When two or three are gathered together acknowledging just how close to defeat they might be, then soon the stirrings of indignation arise. Indignation is a powerful emotion that provides a bridge between passivity and the motivation to embrace intentional activity.

There is a church that is open each day with the expectation that drug addicts, even addicts high on drugs will come in. The power of the holy in that space has the potential to enable the addicted to rekindle the lost hope of being able to free themselves from their addiction; the sense of the holy in that place helping the addict continually to rehearse putting their hand in the hand of their

God as they grapple with their captivity to drugs, searching for the moment when they can say no to drugs, and say no, again and again.[9]

The third example of 'embracing a context in a way that assumes hopeful possibility' might be disputed as being an example of the process of church. Which begs the question, why not? On Sunday 19 October 2008 on Radio Four the morning service came from St Monica's Trust, a resources centre in Westbury on Trym, and the preacher was the Revd Margaret Goodall, Chaplain for Methodist Homes for the Aged. The theme was 'Choose Life' and throughout the service, elderly frail people, including those with dementia, contributed, demonstrating the ways they had come to 'choose life'. I phoned an old old friend later in the day. She is over ninety and ruminates over what is to become of her, dreading the prospect of moving into a residential home. She had lost her fear. By listening to the morning service she had seen the possibility of hope and life being sustained right up to her death. She was sad that St Monica's Trust was too far away for her to consider. 'Oh, but Methodist Homes are just like that, and are all over Britain,' I replied. 'Can you get me some details?' she requested. She had seen the possibility of a hopeful future.

One of the most dreaded features of growing old is the prospect of needing residential care and the possibility of dementia. It is feared more than death itself. In this context, the possibility of a hope-filled future was made manifest through the capacity of Methodist Homes to *enact hope* sufficiently to reassure people of the possibility of deliverance from anxiety, and a hopeful life into the future. Much energy is given to 'fresh expressions' of church, and churches up and down the land are straining to invent something that is different from Sunday-by-Sunday worship, and that has integrity in relation to the Gospel mandate to follow Jesus in his care for the troubled. However, this *fresh expression* is held by the trustees of Methodist Homes for the Aged rather than the Methodist Connexion or the Conference – so does it count as a fresh expression of the process of church? Is it just the issue of

---

9   These two examples the 'holy' being harnessed to help foster positive intent are from my chapter 'Sacred Space in the City', in P. North and J. North (eds), *Sacred Space*, London: Continuum, 2007, p. 130.

governance and ownership that traps our imagination? Might it also be the case that our imagination is too entranced by prestigious and glamorous fresh expressions? Mission to and pastoral care of the slow to die is singularly unglamorous,[10] but it is vitally relevant to those who anticipate becoming frail, which is likely to be most of us.

THEOLOGY FOR RESILIENCE

The process of church for the bothered and bewildered has to combine both pastoral care and mission because, as described earlier in this chapter, the investment of the non-poor in personal competence (as well as the financial investments of the non-poor) has been shaken. I also suggested that the meagre theology which has persisted, despite the chill winds of secularism and mind-numbing materialism, can no longer carry the strain. The pastoral and mission challenge, therefore, is to make grace relevant and new every day. Again the challenge is to the imagination: What shape would such resilient theology take? Where can we learn of it? Who might have pioneered a theological foundation for troubled times? I found it when I was privileged to interview church members living in some of the housing schemes in Glasgow and Edinburgh. Here people have always been under pressure, not just the pressure of the current economic downturn.

For those who have experienced long-lasting poverty and vulnerability, brokenness can become holy ground. It is a blessing to have a new day, although the new day may bring new challenges that can add to one's brokenness. For those who know the reality of long-lasting poverty and brokenness, vulnerability is acknowledged as inescapable. However, it is in this state of vulnerability that mysterious blessings are discovered, and which provide deep reassurance of God's presence. Past experience suggests there is no reason to doubt God's alongsideness and faithfulness into the future. This is the theology of resilience, and the church for the

---

10 Perhaps we all need reminding that harnessing compassion and imagination and commitment on behalf of mill workers and miners was also singularly unglamorous in the eighteenth century.

bothered and bewildered has to make room for such a theology of resilience.

It is too extreme to invite the process of church to abandon investment in success and swap this for recognition of the persistence of vulnerability. Not only would this be too great a somersault, it would also be dishonest, as the inherited process of church has accumulations of power and status that will persist even through the most dismal of times. But nevertheless, the church for the bothered and bewildered cannot allow itself to get caught up in the games of success and competition. There is an alternative, and it is to focus on the goal of being a *contribution*. The pastoral responsibility and mission at the heart of the church process in dystopian times has to see itself as a place of contribution, rather than as an arena for success. The first step involves reflecting on the question 'How will I or the local church be a contribution today?' The willingness to see oneself and the church as a contribution brings an emphasis on relationship with others, and unlike the rewards of status and power that come from 'success', the rewards that come from being a contributor, are deep, enduring and hopeful, and speak of the reality of the abundant economy.[11]

MUTE CHRISTIANS?

The capacity or desire for control is linked with the ability to accumulate and sustain power. 'Control' is the mask which enables those who already have resources to manage scarce resources to their further advantage. The practice of reflection exposes the dynamics of power and control, and this may not be to everyone's taste. Paulo Freire used the term *muteness* to describe the reluctance to engage in reflection[12] (reflection = to ponder and question hard the dynamics operating in relation to one's context). In

---

11   R.S. Zander and B. Zander explore the idea of seeing oneself as a 'contribution' rather than a success, in their book *The Art of Possibility*, London: Penguin, 2000, see pp. 55–65.
12   P. Freire, *Educacao como Pratica da Liberdade*, Rio de Janeiro: Editoria Civilizacao Brasileira, 1967, p. 69.

chapter 2 I suggested that the woman at the well, as a result of her conversation with Jesus, shed her muteness. Being mute means that one's awareness or consciousness is limited to a 'taken-for-granted' view of the world and a devalued sense of self. Furthermore, it is not just individuals that can be mute, but groups and societies also can lose the capacity for critical dialogue. For example, colonialism has been cited as fostering 'muteness' by so shaping the consciousness or awareness of those who are colonised that they become unable to engage in critical dialogue with their context, and unable to see the oppressive relationships to which they are subjected.

Radical educators (educators committed to empowering people to think for themselves) observe that inaction is often the consequence of the experience of muteness. Laziness or failure to engage, which is so often the route by which blame gets put on the less powerful, is a significant outcome of the relationship of domination. Laziness is a defensive reaction against domination. This description, which grows out of observations of colonialism, could be applied to the position and response of congregations in the inherited process of church. Just as the black community in the United States began to see itself as a 'colony', in the sense that political decisions were being made for them by the dominant or mainstream society, so too 'lay' people risk having their discipleship shaped by the interests of those who maintain the dominant process of church. This dynamic may be a contributor to the high number of committed church members, who perceive that to express discipleship more seriously necessitates them embarking on the route to ordination and becoming clericalised.

The new consciousness achieved by black people in the United States was linked with achieving a sense of their history – a sense of being an 'actor' in one's own right. And when one achieves this sense of having made a distinctive contribution to the human enterprise in the past, the likelihood is that one sees the potential to do so in the future. To continue the parallels with lay people in the established denominations, a case could be made that congregations have lost a sense of their (our) history, and with this, have lost a sense of their (our) capacity to make a distinctive contribution to the kingdom of God. Becoming familiar with one's history is a first step towards being an 'actor' in one's own right (i.e. refusing to be trapped by circumstances and embracing intentional activity), and this echoes the concept of *dangerous memories* within liberation theology. A dangerous memory harnesses 'the memory of the past as a critique of the present'[13] to help see that current hopelessness and passivity are not the final word. From these dangerous memories it becomes possible to develop a 'self-consciousness', a reflectiveness that tries to make sense of the dynamics that have contributed to one's habitual behaviour, in order that new possibilities can be achieved.

This no doubt controversial issue about the inhibition of lay people in our current church processes provides the third clue about how to do church in troubled times. The model of church that can equip people to respond with critical awareness in dismal times has to be one that empowers and supports reflection. However, the process of reflection cannot just be directed outward, it is a process that will also put the church itself under scrutiny. If the process of church is able to encourage and sustain reflective practice, then that church will need to be frank about the voracity of churches for people's time and money, to the extent that discipleship risks being reduced to maintaining church life, rather than enacting hope in troubled times. Likewise, the development of the skills of lay people as part of a movement towards *collaborative* ministry will be scrutinised, because this too can be a tactic of the powerful to maintain the status quo. These are difficult, uncomfortable and challenging processes, which may be why many opt for 'muteness'.

As if to exonerate those who occupy positions of power from exercising *wilful* domination, Paulo Freire acknowledges that, despite knowing better, his practice as a teacher continued to reflect the interest of the dominant community. He writes:

> Despite some years of experience as an educator, with urban and rural workers, I still nearly always started out with my world, without further explanation, as if it ought to be the 'south' to which their compass ought to point in giving them their bearings. It was as if my word, my theme, my reading of the world, in themselves, were to be their compass.[14]

---

13 M.C. Grey, *The Outrageous Pursuit of Hope*, London: Darton Longman and Todd, 2000, p. 28.
14 P. Freire, *Pedagogy of Hope*, New York: Continuum, 1996, p. 22.

This admission by this radical educator from the southern hemisphere, endorses the need for each of us to embrace the struggle to see beyond the perceptions offered to us by those in positions of power, and to work to discern for ourselves and develop an imagination that can see things from the perspective of the less powerful.

Even so, there are some things that are best addressed obliquely, because to address them head on is to risk unfortunate and damaging consequences. Debate about the extent to which lay people are exploited and manipulated must surely take place, but cannot constructively be addressed head on. An oblique route that can honourably carry this debate – and achieve much else besides, is to construct a curriculum or syllabus that would enable the equipping of people to *steady the soul when the heart and head are under pressure.* To be able to enact hope in dismal times the nine aptitudes identified earlier in this chapter are important, and these aptitudes are founded on the kind of reflective practice that is fostered by Kolb's learning cycle. One of the potentially fruitful elements of such a syllabus would involve cross-cultural experience. In a globalising world, one of the new deprivations is to be limited to knowledge of only a single culture.

In encountering a culture that is profoundly different from one's own, a host of immediate and enticing challenges are raised. Negotiating the learning curve associated with the nine aptitudes is achieved extraordinarily effectively by twinning with a community in another part of the world. The Church of Scotland has developed a programme called 'Together for a Change', which fosters and continually feeds reflective practice. More than anything, the encounters with those who have little at all materially build confidence in the reality and potency of enduring emotions such as joy, fun, simplicity of life, gratitude. These are the higher emotions that are vital to the economy of abundance. It is noteworthy that this programme aims at involving those from the poorest housing schemes, because so often it is the poorest people in Britain who have least opportunity to partake of a culture different from their own. The international mission societies that once supported hundreds upon hundreds of missionaries are well placed to promote such opportunities that would be extremely valuable to the process of being church for the bothered and bewildered.

LOCAL MATTERS

Although the process of church in troubled times will be fed by cross-cultural encounter, it will also be local, in the sense of working at neighbourhood level. In troubled times one's neighbourhood is potentially a shield against anomie, because neighbours are the ones who deliver (or not) on the values of hospitality and generosity. However, there is another reason why the local, or neighbourhood, is important to the process of church in troubled times, and this relates to the insights of Alistair MacIntyre. In the final gloomy pages of *After Virtue*, which, despite having been written in 1981, resonate strongly with our current dismal mood, MacIntyre compares the then present to the Dark Ages. He suggested that the virtues of morality and civility have been so eroded by the unquestioned effectiveness of accumulating profit, power and status that the challenge becomes one of survival. For MacIntrye, organising one's life around the values of profit, power and status, will not provide a life with meaning or purpose, nor provide an adequate or *sufficient* route to achieve the 'common good'. MacIntyre offers only the single clue as to how to find a way through the grimness. He writes, 'What matters at this stage is the construction of local forms of community within which civility and the intellectual and moral life can be sustained through the new dark ages which are already upon us.'[15]

MacIntrye does not explain the reasons for putting his hope in local forms of community, but one can speculate why it is that at the local level it is possible to enact, or perform hope. It is at the local level where it is possible to harness the imagination as well as commitment to bring other values into play, values that are more conducive to the common good than those of profit, power and status. At other levels of our social organisation (beyond the local) it becomes more and more difficult to counter the potency of the dominant assumption that it is by the accumulation of profit, power and status that one achieves effectiveness in relation to one's aspirations. The local level, although not immune to the dynamics of profit, power and status, provides more scope to imagine and practise a performance that draws on alternative values.

---

15   A. MacIntyre, *After Virtue*, 2nd edn, Notre Dame: University of Notre Dame Press, 1984, p. 263.

This is very relevant to the challenge of developing a process of church for troubled times. It is the local or neighbourhood level that provides the most obliging environment in which to *practice* the enduring and higher emotions that are an essential part of the economy of abundance. It is at the local level where generous and courageous micro-actions can be practised and graced actions risked. It is at the local or neighbourhood level where the imagination can be given full rein, ever aware that as Brueggemann suggests, the poetic imagination prefigures the prophetic imagination which takes the performance to a larger stage.[16] However, a word of caution is needed at this point. Recognising the importance of the local does not give permission to ignore the challenges of globalisation. In particular, we cannot walk away from the fact that 80 per cent of our brothers and sisters across the world are seriously poor, and that this brings destruction and dismay to the *whole* human enterprise. Therefore in commending a local orientation, it must not become parochial, i.e. concerned only with our immediate environment.

MacIntyre put the spotlight on the corrosiveness of the accumulation of profit, power or status becoming the driving forces in personal and corporate life. However, profit and the accumulation of wealth are not particularly strong motivators for people of a religious (and strong ideological) disposition, but the urge for purity can be a potent driver. 'Purity' is what ideologues and fundamentalists seek: i.e. the promotion of their own image of a perfectible future, at all costs. However, psychoanalysis gives short shrift to purity: 'The urge for purity is a direct expression of regressive narcissism, i.e. "a refusal to engage with reality", and as a consequence the "violent obliteration of otherness".'[17] Religion is not alone in its yearning for purity. The urge for purity caused fascist leaders to exterminate those who stood in the way of their strategy for 'progress' and the shaping of a society that would fulfil their ideological dream. Heeding this warning, the process of church for the bothered and bewildered needs to be rooted in imperfection, taking the reality of sin so seriously that 'purity' becomes an impossible aspiration. The church for the bothered and

16 W. Brueggemann, *The Hopeful Imagination*, London: SCM Press, 1986.
17 S. Frosh, *Identity Crisis: Modernity, Psychoanalysis and the Self*, London: Macmillan, 1991, p. 94.

bewildered needs continually to acknowledge human frailty to the extent that perfection is never expected; otherwise the wonderful liberating generosity of being treated better than we deserve, this ultimate 'alternative performance' that Jesus offers, is unnecessary.

In outlining the characteristics of the process of church that can enact hope in troubled times, there is one final task: to return to the controversial claim that formulaic faith has to be superseded by a greater commitment to reflective practice. In chapter 2 I suggested that we risk falling prey to a new version of gnosticism if we persist with the formulas of our faith, that are meaningful to those who have been formed in the faith, but which are inscrutable or alienating to others. In other words, preoccupation with doctrine and dogma makes God so incredible to people that we risk failure to deliver the inclusive grace, or generosity, that is the motivating energy at the heart of God's love for his creation. It would be foolish to dismiss doctrine, but there needs to be honesty about the hurdle that is presented when people are invited to believe certain 'truths', when their need, especially in dystopian times, is to pursue a profound desire for meaning. The church for the bothered and bewildered will be one that shifts the balance from investment in 'belief' to acknowledging the everyday relevance and cathartic and energising nature of the story of Jesus who shows us how to live.

Our faith is rooted in a person who said 'I am ... the truth.' Jesus did not say 'I will speak true words to you' or 'I will tell you about the truth.' Instead, the claim Jesus makes is that he embodies truth in his person. Palmer comments that 'Those who sought truth were invited into relationship with him and through him with the whole community of the human and non-human world.'[18] This view of truth rejects the idea that truth is an objective 'out there'. Rather truth is something that comes to be known through encounter and relationship and a commitment to reflect on these. Palmer concludes that, 'If what we *know* is an abstract, impersonal, apart from us, it cannot be truth, for truth involves a vulnerable, faithful, and risk filled interpenetration of the knower and the known.'[19]

---

18 Parker J. Palmer, *To Know as We Are Known*, San Francisco: Harper Row, 1983, p. 47.
19 Ibid., p. 49.

HOPE SPRINGS UP NOT TRICKLES DOWN

The conceptual coherence to which doctrine aspires, is not something that is valued by postmodern people, who are well aware that the world is too complex to fit into the neat categories of scientific formulae, analytic reports and other products of the intellect. Reflective practice acknowledges that insight cannot be achieved by reason alone, because honest thinking requires more than just clarity of thought – it calls for both courage and commitment. This is particularly important in dystopian times when people detect the whiff of a pie that has gone rotten, and the even more pungent odour of denial. In such a context, the offer of honesty can be a holy and sacred offering.

People know in their heart of hearts that we live in the midst of tremendous dishonesty and denial, but there is an impasse, because cynicism is such that no one can be trusted to say how it is. In recent history, there is an example of the process of church that did find a way to achieve courageous honesty and enact hope; it is the story of churches in East Berlin at the time when East Berlin was separated from West Berlin by the Berlin Wall. For decades television footage showed the wall surrounded by furlongs of barbed wire, lit by giant spotlights, and patrolled night and day, and the newscasts told of how those who dared to approach the Wall had been shot on sight.

In those days of the Berlin Wall, the churches in East Berlin were the gathering places of tiny numbers of people, often the most vulnerable and broken people, the very elderly, and scarcely viable eccentrics. The churches were tolerated by the East German authorities because it was clear that the churches were so weak they carried no threat to the power of the massive German Democratic Republic, so the policy was to leave them be, and allow them to die of their own accord. Except that this didn't happen. It didn't happen because those churches in East Berlin dared to hanker after truth. Those frail, insignificant churchgoers persisted in trying to read the signs of the times, and persisted in that strange and apparently old-fashioned liturgical poetry that spoke of a different, hopeful future. Imperceptibly, others began to join them, attracted to the honest search for truth that characterised those worn-down, scorned churches – for no other agency in East Germany had the poetry that could express the growing awareness that 'the pie was rotten', that the system wasn't working.

The broken-down and often mocked churches had developed a profound, mournful prayerfulness – because what else could they do? Prayerfulness was the hallmark of the growth of possibility, and as the numbers attending the churches in East Berlin grew, so too did their prayerfulness. Prayerfulness, as well as helping people to rise above entrapment by circumstance, also contributes to exquisite timing. Through their courageous honesty and committed prayerfulness those in the churches sensed when to act. They noted that increasingly, as the traffic was held up to allow party officials in their Volvos to speed across road junctions, people risked leaning on their horns to express their frustration; muteness was dissolving. News from Poland prompted reflection on whether the moment had come for them to begin their time of commitment and passion, when they knew they had to walk towards the wall, cutting back the barbed wire as they walked and wielding their sledgehammers to break down the wall. It was the old women of the churches, too frail to wield or carry sledgehammers, who led the way.

Studs Terkel, the American oral historian, made a point of listening to those whom others were inclined to ignore. This commitment to listening well and listening long led him to conclude that 'Hope has never trickled down. It has always sprung up,' [20]and this observation provides the final clue about the process of church for troubled times.

---

20   S. Terkel, *Hope Dies Last*, New York: The New Press, 2003, p. xv.

Index